D0184775

SR

GURKHA
BROTHERHOOD

GURKHA
BROTHERHOOD

A Story of Childhood and War

CAPTAIN KAILASH LIMBU

Michael O'Mara Books Limited

First published in Great Britain in 2021 by
Michael O'Mara Books Limited
9 Lion Yard
Tremadoc Road
London SW4 7NQ

A CIP catalogue record for this book is available from the British Library.

Every effort has been made to identify the owners of copyright material reproduced in this book. The author would like to apologize for any omissions and will be pleased to incorporate missing acknowledgements in future editions.

Papers used by Michael O'Mara Books Limited are natural, recyclable products made from wood grown in sustainable forests. The manufacturing processes conform to the environmental regulations of the country of origin.

ISBN: 978-1-78929-257-2 in hardback print format
ISBN: 978-1-78929-259-6 in ebook format

1 2 3 4 5 6 7 8 9 10

Designed and typeset by Design 23
Printed and bound by CPI Group (UK) Ltd, Croydon, CR0 4YY

www.mombooks.com

MIX
Paper from
responsible sources
FSC® C020471

*This book is dedicated to my dearest mother –
I know she is watching me through success and
struggle. To all my family members and friends who
were there for me, and to all my unforgotten beloved
brothers who lost their lives in war and peace.*

CONTENTS

INTRODUCTION

In 2016, I completed the last of five active service tours of Afghanistan with the British Army. As a soldier in the 2nd Battalion, the Royal Gurkha Rifles, I was in the front line of the fighting in Helmand Province between 2006 and 2014. I was also, in 2016, deployed in the Afghan capital, Kabul. On dangerous resupply missions and offensive patrols, we Gurkhas came under frequent attack from Taliban fighters and other insurgents. None of us will ever forget what we went through together. It formed a bond of brotherhood between us that nothing and no one can break.

When I returned home it was not to Nepal, the mountainous country in faraway South Asia where we Gurkhas grew up. It was to the UK – to Folkestone in Kent. Sir John Moore Barracks in Shorncliffe Garrison in Folkestone is the base of the Royal Gurkha Rifles in Britain. In 2016, I lived there in MoD quarters with my wife and two young children. I am a man with two homes. I hold both countries dear in my heart.

My childhood home was very different from the modern military quarters at Shorncliffe. It was built of mud and stone on the steep slope of a Himalayan valley. Its walls were brightly painted and sweet-smelling flowers grew around it. We had no electricity, no television, no modern gadgets at all. My mother cooked on an open fire and it was one of my jobs, when I was a kid, to collect dry firewood from the forest. I have a memory that still makes me feel guilty: of my mother in tears because the firewood I had collected that day was damp and would not light.

My mountain village was a beautiful place to grow up. I had lots of friends and we had many adventures. But it was not a fairytale. The Himalayas could be an unpredictable environment. Long before I joined the British Army and fought in Afghanistan, I learned that fate can be cruel and life sometimes takes a wrong turn. Even as a child I was no stranger to danger and death.

In the first few weeks after returning from my final deployment in Afghanistan, memories of what happened there were still fresh in my mind. Sometimes they gave me bad nights, when I could not sleep or woke up crying. Other times I felt a surge of pride and warmth at what we had achieved. But these memories were slowly fading.

One day I was sitting on the sofa in the sitting room in Folkestone thinking about the past. Not just Afghanistan but my childhood growing up in the Himalayas, which seemed like a different world and lifetime. A war film was on TV, the kind of film that makes war look quick and easy. In front of me my two children were playing. And I was really looking forward to the dinner my wife, Sumitra, was preparing in the kitchen next door – *momos* (dumplings) stuffed with pork and chicken. Then an idea floated into my head: get these memories down on paper while I could.

The idea excited me. That night I could not sleep so I got up, grabbed a sheet of paper and began to write. The words poured out of me, the childhood joys and scrapes, the times in Afghanistan when I feared I would not live to see the sun set at the end of the day. Some faces came up again and again in my mind. They belonged to the several Gurkha brothers I lost, dear friends who stood shoulder-to-shoulder with me in the heat of battle.

The project got more serious. In spare moments and during those sleepless nights I sat in front of my computer, and built a bigger and bigger picture of my life. This book is the result. It is a tribute to my family and the wonderful upbringing they gave me. It is a memorial to brave friends who fell in the killing fields of Afghanistan. It is the story, above all, of a boy from a simple background who laid his life on the line for his adopted country and his Gurkha brothers.

In the battlefield scenes I do not try to give a wider military or historical perspective. They are how I remember them – how they looked and felt at the time, with the bullets flying and the adrenaline pumping. Inevitably, others who were there may remember things slightly differently. But this is *my* reality. I dedicate it to the ones who did not make it. I hope and believe, with all my heart and soul, that in some corner of heaven they are looking down and reading it with you.

CHAPTER 1

ON MY WAY

My home was – and still is, in my heart – a village called Khebang in the green foothills of the Himalayas in the northeast of Nepal. The majestic snow-white peak of Kanchenjunga – at 8,500 m, the third-highest mountain in the world – rises about 48 km away. Our little community of fewer than 2,000 people lived in colourful, wooden houses, surrounded by forests of tall trees and rhododendrons that are far bigger and wilder than the rhododendrons you get in the UK.

I liked to explore these forests. Sometimes it was just to play with friends from the village, looking for insects and fruit, and scaring each other with stories of the ghosts who lived in the trees. But I also had important family tasks to perform in the forest. I collected firewood and mushrooms, and I took the family's goats and cows there so they could graze on the grasses and plants.

On these outings I went deeper and deeper into the forest, exploring unfamiliar areas. I would frequently lose my way and lose track of the animals, who liked to push on in search of lusher vegetation. Sometimes it took me a long time to find them. On one occasion I had been looking and calling for hours and it was getting dark.

The forest at night was not a place where anyone went willingly. Evil spirits emerged, looking for boys like me to harm. I was so fed up and scared that I just sat down among the trees. I put my head in my hands and cried, imagining the bad ghosts, imagining having to explain to my parents that I had lost the cattle – if I lived long enough to tell the tale.

I cried so much I thought my eyes would never see properly again. Then I heard a noise nearby that frightened me out of my wits. A ghost! I leapt up and began to run, tripping and staggering through the undergrowth. The ghost followed, I could hear it. I risked a look back – and saw the cattle following me. I had been running from exactly what I was looking for!

From that moment I felt a bond with the cattle, and I believe they felt a similar attachment to me. Every day they would wait patiently for me to come, their ears pricking up as I approached. We had some real adventures together.

Being in the forest was not like a walk in the British countryside, with its squirrels and acorns. As well as the ghosts, there were dangerous wild animals: the wolves, snow leopards and black bears. My senses were always on high alert, a discipline that would stand me in good stead many years later in the killing zones of Afghanistan. At the same time I had my trusty *khukuri* knife to fight off ferocious beasts. With its distinctive, curved blade the khukuri is both weapon and tool for the Gurkha, a symbol of his home and culture.

In fact, though I had plenty of sightings, usually out of the corner of my eye, I was never attacked by wild animals, unless you count leeches. It is true what they say, creatures *are* generally more frightened of you than you are of them. The real dangers lurked elsewhere. The beautiful mountain scenery that surrounded us could turn dark and deadly in the blink of an eye.

These hills are threaded with rivers, rapids and waterfalls. The biggest river in the region is the Tamor, one of Nepal's most treacherous, which drains the melt waters of Kanchenjunga. But smaller ones are all around. Khebang village is situated about 4 miles from a river we called the Tawa, with waterfalls and rapids that could be deadly in torrential rain.

When I was growing up quite a few villagers lost their lives in the Tawa. Some were just tending their animals or crops and were unlucky to lose their footing. Some were drunk. One was a mother carrying her small child in a basket. She fell 12 m into the churning waters. Both drowned. My parents drilled into me how dangerous was the Tawa, so I learned every path and route around it. I knew the terrain above its banks like the back of my hand. I was confident it would never get me.

The ghosts were a different matter. Fear of ghosts and witches was not just a childhood thing that people grew out of. Many adults in the village also believed there were evil spirits out there that would kill you, given half the chance.

The village was surrounded by several graveyards and these were thought to be gathering places of ghosts.

If someone really wanted to scare the wits out of you, they would tell you that the *murkatta* were coming to get you. These ghosts liked to drink human blood and were the most terrible of all. They did not need the cloak of night to operate; they could walk around in the middle of the day. They were headless yet had some sort of light on their shoulders, so you could see them coming from far away. But sometimes they just appeared out of nowhere. Then they would kill you.

My mother told me that they did this by taking your *saato*. This roughly translates as 'soul', but it has an additional meaning – a protective power that prevents a person being taken over by supernatural forces. I heard plenty of stories of people who had been killed by the murkatta. As you can imagine, I was terrified of coming across them, and tried to avoid any dark and spooky places, especially those graveyards.

Sometimes, when I was out on my own, I would sense something. Then my body would feel numb, my head as if it were expanding like a balloon. My ears picked up strange noises that I could not explain. Then I would pinch myself, spit on my body and recite mantras that my father and grandfather had taught me in case I were attacked by ghosts. After such a fright I kept looking behind me as I walked home to make sure I was not being followed. This was what my childhood was like. I grew up in a beautiful place, life was simple and I was happy. But danger and disaster were never far away, even if they were sometimes only in your own imagination.

The village was very remote. We had to walk for two days just to reach a road where we could pick up a bus. Then it was another day on the bus before you got to a town of any size. There was no telephone connection until I was much older. So we really did feel cut off from the outside world but there was one connection we did have. Every so often a passenger jet would fly over, high in the blue sky, shining like silver. To me this was as amazing as seeing a space ship. I would watch it all the way till it disappeared over the horizon, wondering where it came from, where it was going and who the people on board were. Once, when I was out in the fields, I was so busy following one of these planes with my eyes that I fell over and broke my ankle!

Little did I know then that, one day, I would be flying in such a plane to start a new life on the other side of the world. Joining the Gurkhas certainly changed my life and, looking back, it is easy to say that it was always a likely outcome for me. After all, the Gurkha tradition was in my blood. My grandfather served as a British Gurkha in India. One uncle was in the Queen's Own Gurkha Logistic Regiment (QOGLR) and several others were in the Gurkha Contingent of the Singapore Police Force.

My grandfather was the biggest influence. He had an old photograph of himself in uniform in India that always fascinated me. It was blurry and you could not make out that much but I could see that he was barefoot, that he had a long moustache and I really noticed his rifle.

He still had the rifle at home. I used to admire it as he told me about the principles of marksmanship, how you had to focus and concentrate and slow your breathing before firing. I really wanted to have a go but he said I was too young. As we tended the cattle in the fields he talked to me a lot about his days as a Gurkha soldier. We would sit down in the shade of a big tree and he would tell me what a good shot he was. He also told me about the application tests for joining the Gurkhas and how hard they were, but that he did very well, especially in the running exercises.

From a young age part of me wanted to become an elite soldier like my grandfather. But the story was more complicated. I also thought of becoming a doctor. If there had been a doctor in our village when I was growing up there is no doubt many lives would have been saved. From a Western perspective it was a very unhealthy environment. Many people died from simple illnesses and infections that anyone, with a basic medical knowledge and basic medical supplies, could have prevented or cured. When I was born in 1981, a mother in a village like mine stood only a 50:50 chance of surviving childbirth. In fact my birth went smoothly, so my mum told me proudly. But she was not so lucky when she had my sister, Gudiya, eleven years later.

I remember how frightening it was. She had just given birth on the verandah of the house (traditionally women are not permitted to give birth in the family house itself). When she went inside she suddenly fell unconscious and collapsed on the floor. My father and some villagers tried to pick her up. I tried to push her up from underneath, but I was not tall or strong enough to help.

She was losing a lot of blood. She stayed unconscious for what seemed like an eternity. The *dhami*, the local shaman-priest was saying prayers and asking God to save her life (our religion is a mix of Hinduism and a shamanistic faith called Kirat that is local to the eastern Himalayas). My aunties brought a bowl of water and were splashing it in her face. I really thought we had lost her. I was already thinking what it would be like from now on for my sister and me to grow up without a mother. She came through in the end but it was touch-and-go, and I never forgot those moments.

Later, when my sister was about four, Mum was frequently ill. Sometimes she had difficulty breathing. Sometimes she had bad stomach pains. By this time my father was away from home, working on construction sites in the Persian Gulf. So, at fifteen years old, I was the man of the house and felt responsible for Mum's health. I could not bear to watch her suffering, and each time she cried out I thought she was dying.

The only thing I could do was call the dhami. Several times I ran to his house in the middle of the night. It was about 4 km away and I was terrified of the dark, of the ghosts that might be waiting in the shadows to kill me. In one hand I carried a torch of lighted bamboo sticks and in the other my khukuri. I would bring the dhami back, and he would recite prayers and sprinkle rice and water to ward off the evil spirits. But I knew this was no substitute for proper medical care.

Another significant thing happened around this time. My father was involved in a very bad car accident in the Gulf and spent twenty-one days in intensive care. We did not know about this at the time; the only contact we had was by letter, and these took ages to arrive. It was nearly four months after the accident that we found out, when a letter arrived from my father's friend. It made me think even harder of what I could do to make my parents' lives better.

Meanwhile, my mother was finding it harder and harder to cope. With my father away she had to work extra hard in the fields during the day, even in the wet season when the rain came down in floods. We had to make sure to plant at the right time and look after the crops, or there would not be any food to harvest. I helped her, of course, but I also had to go to school. And I was not always the perfect son that I tried to be.

I was an adolescent boy with lots of energy and a bit of a wild side. I really liked playing sports and I was very competitive, especially in volleyball; when I was a new Gurkha recruit we played volleyball as part of our fitness training and I was known as one of the best players – no one could return the ball when I spiked it over the net. I also started staying out late playing with my friends and Mum got worried. She had reason to be. Sometimes things got out of hand with my friends and we started fighting each other using sticks and stones, and even khukuris. Some boys got badly injured.

Then, when I got home in the dark, I would find Mum still working and feel really guilty for leaving her on her own. She worked every evening, distilling a homemade alcoholic drink called *raksi* that she sold to villagers to make money. It was a hard life by any standards, and she was frequently ill and permanently tired. I was worrying more and more about her, and one night I lay in bed unable to sleep.

Outside dogs were barking and our dog, Denney, joined in. He was lovely, part of the family. When we were working in the fields we would leave my sister asleep in her basket and Denney watched over her. When she woke up he would bark to let us know. But he was so annoying that night. His damned barking was keeping me awake.

I started thinking about Mum and Dad. My mum could not go on much longer like this. And Dad had almost died in the car crash and his health would never be the same again. I needed to help them. By this point I had just finished my final year, Year 10, at school and obtained my Leaving Certificate with the top grade. My plan was to study science at college, then go on to study medicine. But it was a long road and it would cost a lot of money. My parents would have to work even harder to earn the money to support me until I qualified.

Another possible plan was to get married, so my mum would have a new generation to help around the house. Boys and girls my age in the surrounding villages were already getting together. This happened in the local *melas* (bazaars), where people from different castes – not just Limbu but Rai, Tamang and Gurung – came from all over to shop for food, clothing and jewellery, and to sing and dance.

One of the dances is called *dhan nach* and people of any age can do it. For the young it is a chance to meet members of the opposite sex. When doing the dance boys and girls are allowed to hold hands, so long as they are not related. They also sing a traditional song called *palam*, which is like a duet or a call-and-response between the boy and girl. Lots of marriages begin with the dhan. I really enjoyed it and met lots of nice girls. My parents and grandparents were definitely quite keen for me to get married, but I decided it was too soon. It would interfere with my career. The question was, what would that career be?

So that night when I could not sleep, lying there listening (again) to my barking dog, I knew what I had to do. I would follow in the footsteps of my grandfather and uncle and become a Gurkha soldier. It would make my parents proud, and it would solve the family's financial problems. All Gurkhas send money back to their families. I would be able to build them a house near a city, where they could have a better and easier life with access to proper medical facilities.

In the morning I told Mum, 'I'm going to join the Gurkhas.' It would not be as easy as that, of course. I knew there were many difficult steps. She was delighted but worried for me. My school record was good and I was physically strong, but she thought I needed feeding up to make me stronger. She made me eat raw eggs; they were warm and slimy but I shut my eyes, took a deep breath and swallowed them whole.

We spent long evenings talking about the future. I told her I would build a new house for them, that she would not have to work so hard and Dad would not have to work abroad. This made her happy, I could see. Once a week, early in the morning, she took me to the shrine dedicated to Pathibara Devi, the goddess sacred to the Limbu people, in a cave near the house. Here we prayed for good fortune, good health and for my future success. The prayers helped me. I had more energy, studied better. I felt calm and confident.

I had to go through three selection boards in my quest to be a Gurkha soldier. The first was in a village a few hours' walk from Khebang. I was one of 600 from the surrounding area who turned up. We had a medical, did physical exercises (sit-ups, pull-ups, a run) and had an academic assessment. Just twenty of us got through to the next stage, in Taplejung, the main town in the area. Here the odds were really daunting – more than a thousand applicants for fourteen places.

There were more tests and exercises, but what I remember is the interview. I was asked why I wanted to be a Gurkha, so of course I mentioned all the family connections. That did not seem to impress them. Then I said I liked fighting and guns and that seemed to do the trick. I got through to the final board in Pokhara.

At this point I found myself at a crossroads in my life. On the sensible assumption that I might not make it through the Gurkha selection process, I had kept the medical options open by keeping my place at college to study science. But did I want to cure people – or fight them? It was an odd choice. In the end it was made for me.

Shortly before I went to Pokhara for the final selection, my dad returned from the Persian Gulf after two-and-a-half years away. It was an emotional homecoming. He looked older, more tired; he had been through a hell of a lot. Of course he told me how grown-up and tall I was. He was so proud to hear about my success in the first two Gurkha selection boards.

And now just the big one was left.

On the morning that I left for Pokhara, Mum placed pots full of water on either side of the door to bring me luck. Mum, Dad and Gudiya stood on one side, my grandparents on the other. I bowed down and touched their feet (except Gudiya's – you only do it to your elders) as a gesture of respect, and then they blessed me and wished me luck.

Everyone was crying, including me. In fact suddenly I did not want to leave. I wanted to just stay with them and carry on as before. I think I realized that where I was going, and what I was about to do, would change my life forever; that nothing would ever be the same after I had set off. Eventually, I pulled myself away. I had everything I needed in a small backpack. I gave a final wave and was gone. My childhood ended in that moment.

It took me two days to walk to the nearest bus station and another two days on buses, travelling west, first to the city of Dharan then on to Pokhara. On that journey I had plenty of time to think about my future and wonder what I was getting into. And when I finally got to the British Gurkha Camp I just wanted to turn round and go back home again.

I was so homesick in those first few days. This was in pre-internet and mobile phone days and there were no public telephones, no way of contacting the family. In any case it was forbidden to get in touch with them. My 'home' for the next month was a big room with more than a hundred hopefuls living and sleeping in it. That number gradually got smaller as more and more candidates were eliminated, and in that sense it was like the *Big Brother* house!

This was my first experience living and working in a group. Up to that point I had thought of myself as an individual. Sure, I had friends and we did things together, but I always went home to my own house at the end of the day. Now I was a very small part of a much bigger picture. The other candidates came from all over Nepal. Many were from the big cities and seemed to know much more than me.

We were of different castes and ages. We were tall and short, spoke different languages and had different customs but we quickly learned to be tolerant, respectful and disciplined towards each other. And gradually, as we went through things together, I began to look on them as my brothers.

There were about 800 of us at the beginning of this final selection. We were competing for about 250 places, and each day we were put through a series of tests designed to measure our physical health and abilities, leadership qualities, character, initiative, and so on. The most infamous of these challenges had to be the *doko* race.

A *doko* is a basket used in the mountains for carrying wood or rice. You wear it on your shoulders with a strap around your forehead, and the key is to keep it balanced. For the test it was loaded with a sandbag or rock weighing about 36 kilos (it's slightly less nowadays) and we had to run a 6 km course that included a steep hill, which made balancing it very tricky. This is the test that everyone fears. I knew I was fairly strong as I was used to carrying heavy loads in the village, but I had not used a doko very much and certainly not in a race like this.

In the end I just kept going. The hill was the worst part. I was so keen to get to the top first that I nearly burst my lungs. I used so much energy on the hill that a few candidates passed me in the rest of the race but I still did well, and that was my approach to all the challenges. As candidates were eliminated day by day I just kept my head down, slept well, concentrated and did my best. And each morning I got up early to pray at the temple near the camp. Once again, I'm sure this helped to keep my head clear and focused.

After nearly three weeks of this we were down to the final elimination. The remaining 300 were instructed to pack their bags and assemble on the parade square. As we sat and waited you could feel the tension. After all this time and effort, and having got this far, some of us were going home with nothing to show for it (though many who narrowly lost out would re-apply the following year).

The Deputy Recruiting Officer appeared with a list of names and began to read them out. Each time the candidate stood up, picked up his bag and moved to the side of the group, where a new group formed. I was so nervous that I got confused. Were the names being called the successful or the rejects? My heart was thumping. I closed my eyes. I prayed. After ten minutes there were more candidates standing in the new group than still sitting, like me, in the middle. It was obvious – the names being called were the ones who had been selected.

He was not reading them out in alphabetical order, so I kept hoping. And our group in the middle was getting smaller.

I convinced myself I had not made it. I was already wondering what I had done wrong and deciding I would come back and try again next year when I heard 'Kailash Limbu!' I was one of the 230 selected from 32,000 initial applicants in cities, towns and villages across Nepal.

I jumped up, grabbed my bag. I was seventeen-and-a-half years old and I was on my way in life. All sorts of feelings flooded through me but the main one was: I can't wait to tell my mum. How proud she'll be!

CHAPTER 2

BIRTHDAY IN HELL

There were so many dangerous days in Afghanistan – days when we were pinned down and fighting for our lives – that they tend to blur together. Yet some stand out, like 8 March 2008 because it was my birthday, and also my daughter Alisa's birthday. In my village we are superstitious about birthdays and believe that if you are ill on your birthday, you will die. I did not feel ill, but I did have a real sense of foreboding as the bullets and bombs rained down on us.

The reasons for the deployment of the British Armed Forces in Afghanistan – as part of the International Security Assistance Force (ISAF) led by NATO – are many and varied and, to be honest, it is not my place to explain them. As a serving soldier

I took my orders, protected the men under my control and observed Rules of Engagement (ROE), showing respect to the civilian population and ruthlessness to the enemy when needed.

In 2008, I was based at FOB (Forward Operating Base) Delhi, a former agricultural college in the Garmsir district of Helmand Province. The section I was in charge of had been deployed south of the base by 3 CH 47 on a clear-and-search mission. At full company strength we were advancing on enemy positions from behind some shot-up houses, backed up by Jackal protected patrol tactical vehicles.

The military loves acronyms (as you might have noticed), and you are going to have to get used to seeing plenty in my descriptions of battlefield engagements. On this occasion an ISTAR (Intelligence, Surveillance, Target Acquisition and Reconnaissance) asset had just pinpointed the location of the enemy, in a cluster of nearby buildings surrounded by trees. Before we could react they had targeted us with mortars.

In response, we hit them with our GPS-guided Multiple Launch Rocket System (GMLRS). These missiles are as effective as old-fashioned mortar bombs, but far more accurate fired from 40 km away, making us have to clear the airspace. The noise was deafening; the ground shook, the impact burst a column of earth, smoke and debris 90 m into the clear blue sky. There for a split second it stayed, as if suspended in time and space. Then the soil and pebbles came drumming down on us.

The soldier next to me, Rifleman (Rfn) Bipen, yelled in triumph: 'Bloody hell! Take some of that!' The adrenaline was flowing through all of us. 'Did we get 'em?' shouted Rfn Rabin. Rfn Dipendra chipped in with, 'Bastards! You try to kill us, we'll wipe you out!'

Bipen, Rabin and Dipendra were three of my *bhaiharu*. This is a useful Gorkhali (or Nepalese) word that I will be using fairly frequently, *bhai* meaning 'junior' or 'younger' and *haru* indicating 'more than one'. So they were my junior colleagues, subordinate to me in terms of rank. And they referred to me, in turn, as *guruji*, a term of respect used for someone senior in age or rank and taken from the word for teacher.

As my bhaiharu let off steam I ran and crawled across a field towards a wall peppered with shell holes, hoping to get a good view of the enemy through the gaps. It was tough going. The field was rough, the heat near-intolerable and then I finally reached the cover of the wall. As I angled my body to position my eye behind one of the holes, I heard a single round and dust exploded in my face and eyes. *'Jhatha!'* (A Nepali word, roughly translated as 'Bloody hell!'). A near miss.

A random thought hit me. Back in the UK my daughter would be missing her father, on this special day of all days. Too young to understand where I was and why I could not be with her, she would be puzzled and hurt by her dad's absence.

I lifted the rifle's scope to my eye and risked another look. The firing was coming from two groups of enemy fighters in the tree-line. I aimed back at them but, however hard I tried, I could not align the shot properly – my breath was coming in heavy bursts after getting across the field. I could not slow my pumping heart.

Then a voice close by: 'Guruji, guruji! Please confirm location of enemy.' This was my 2IC (second-in-command), LCpl (Lance Corporal) Dik. By this time the rest of my section had crawled across the field and joined me in the shelter of the pockmarked wall. More incoming. The enemy's rounds pinged off it, sending up mini-explosions of dust and earth.

'Section watch your front,' I shouted. 'About three hundred and fifty metres, three o'clock, houses at the bottom of the tree-line. *Enemy*!' I gave the target indication. My section started firing. I watched tracer rounds find the enemy firing points. A blaze of lead followed. 'Kill the bastards!' yelled Dipendra.

The noise of rapid weapon fire was joined by something else. Louder, bigger. For a moment I had no idea what it was. Then I turned round and saw that two Jackals had opened up behind us with their heavy machine guns. With a range of more than 1.6 km those weapons are serious killers.

Meanwhile, I was feeling exposed as the magazine on my gun had run out. 'Ammo, ammo,' I shouted, warning my comrades to cover me while I re-loaded. I did not hang about. 'Back in,' I confirmed. Then I crawled parallel to the wall, aiming for a gap that would give me a more complete view. My section fell in behind.

The gap was what we needed. Yes, it made us clear targets in the enemy's gunsights, but it gave us a great arc of fire. Bipen arrived at my shoulder. The rest of the section joined us and we opened up in a blizzard of noise and yells. This was it. The exhilaration, the terror, the chaos of contact. In those moments you feel unstoppable. You know your firepower is greater, more effective, more accurate. How can the enemy withstand it?

Then the enemy seemed to melt away. We knew by now there were lots of them, divided into two groups, but I could no longer identify their location in the tree-line. Sporadic fire was coming from one or two insurgents, riddling the wall next to us with holes, but the rest had ghosted off.

The frustration was overwhelming. I could barely stop myself dashing across the open ground between us and grabbing those guys by the neck. My fingers itched to draw my khukuri. The idea of knifing them really was very attractive.

Instead, I stood up in the gap in the wall and started firing from an upright position, not caring that I was a clear target. One of the enemy suddenly appeared in my rifle sight, in a building at the bottom of the tree-line, and returned fire.

I was blazing away but accurate fire was not easy. Not only was it the heat of battle, with one's life on the line in the event of a single false move. But standing up is not the ideal firing position, and the enemy was at least 300 m away. It was a tough ask to put him down. Then my bhaiharu also spotted him and together we put up a barrage of rounds. That seemed to concentrate his mind and he retreated out of sight to the rear of the building.

Through the rifle sight I continued to scan the building, and it was only now that I realized the extent of the damage inflicted by the GMLRS. Smoke still rose from where they had landed, completely destroying the compound walls. The devastation ... The enemy had surely perished or sustained serious injuries under the onslaught of those missiles. No wonder they had apparently disappeared.

The threat, though, had not been removed. It was imperative we kept up a momentum, moving forward as fast and as safely as possible, clearing the enemy as we advanced. By PRR (Personal Role Radio, a transmitter-receiver used on the battlefield) I instructed my bhaiharu to get ready to move. Behind us, the entire platoon and company were following.

We set off along a rubble-strewn road, swiftly moving in single-file formation and in zigzags to make us harder targets. Leading the way were my trusted scouts, Rabin and Dipendra, with me following and the rest of my section behind. Our goal was a group of three buildings directly ahead. The road provided the only route there, but it was a dangerous channel to use and we were in a state of heightened alert, scanning 360 degrees as we ran.

To either side were compound walls up to 2.5 m high. If a grenade was lobbed over that'd be it. No escape. We were also acutely aware of the threat of IEDs (Improvised Explosive Devices, i.e. homemade bombs planted at the roadside). There was a strong wind blowing that day, whipping up the dust, covering any signs of recent disturbance in the ground.

And there was another factor. It was one of the hottest days I can recall in that baking hot region. Sweat was pouring off my forehead into my eyes. But I could not wipe it away, I could not allow my hand to leave my weapon for a split second. It is in those split seconds of inattention that soldiers lose their lives.

Suddenly, about 80 m short of a T-junction, Rabin and Dipendra stopped moving. My PRR crackled with Rabin's voice. 'Fresh signs of digging, possible IEDs,' he reported. I joined him, followed his pointing finger. Definite signs of disturbance in the ground, consistent with recently buried landmines. Via PRR, I passed on this information to the rest of my section and to the Platoon Commander, Lt Crawley.

Silence. Our advance had stalled. Everyone was waiting for me to make a decision on how to proceed. Should we sweep the ground using a metal detector and clear the booby traps? We were in a highly exposed position, with nowhere to hide. In the time it'd take to defuse the IEDs we would be sitting ducks.

I looked again at the signs on the ground. On second viewing I had my doubts. The disturbance was a bit too obvious, with no attempt at camouflage – as if it was meant to be seen. This was a Taliban tactic. They had learned the drill we used for identifying IEDs. We looked out for VAs (Vulnerable Areas) and, within those, VPs (Vulnerable Points), places where IEDs would be likely to cause maximum damage. Anything suspicious, we swept it.

The roadway was certainly a VA; the T-junction an obvious VP. It looked to me like they had faked signs of IEDs on the roadside to draw us into an ambush. At that moment my suspicions were confirmed. The shooting started. I flattened myself in the very shallow ditch next to the road but there was nearly no cover. Nowhere to hide. We – myself and the seven brothers under my command – were caught in a death trap.

There was no chance of lifting our heads to return fire. Bullets were flying over our heads and striking the ground around us. We were completely pinned down. If this were a boxing match we would be on the ropes, taking blow after blow. About to get knocked out. Without doubt it was one of the most dangerous situations I had been in.

In those moments I really thought my time was up. I was expecting the fatal bullet any second. In fact I wondered if I had already received it, had just seconds live. Then I remembered it was my birthday. I was going to die on my birthday!

No chance. Survival instinct kicked in. I tried to flatten my body even closer to the ground, if that were possible, imagining myself making a smaller and smaller target. The dust probably helped. I was covered in it. The sweat continued dripping off my forehead, and then I risked a look up. Ahead of me, the enemy's rounds were landing frighteningly close to Rabin and Dipendra, glued flat on the ground.

Then a new noise. A smoke trail, a deafening explosion close by. I recognized it straightaway. 'Bloody hell. RPG! RPG!' I yelled. The Rocket Propelled Grenade was one of the Taliban's deadliest weapons – fired from the shoulder by a single insurgent, it was so devastating it could even destroy armoured vehicles. What it could do to human flesh did not bear thinking about.

Luckily it landed on the top of the compound wall to the side of us.

By now we had been pinned down in the same spot for three minutes. In the kind of life-threatening ambush we found ourselves in I had established my SOP – Standard Operating Procedure – for the section, based on previous combat experience. That was to wait two or three minutes before moving. This was because the enemy would be expecting us to move, just waiting to gun us down if we tried to run for cover. Their ambush would have been well planned, and hours if not days in the preparation. They would have picked the firing positions with the best views and arcs of fire. Magazines would be filled, with extra ammunition on hand. All they had to do was sit back and wait for us to arrive.

All this was running through my head. What we had to do – somehow – was find cover and suppress the enemy fire with fire of our own. But, more than three minutes into the ambush, we had not managed to return a single round. I was seriously alarmed for the safety of my bhaiharu.

Due to the flying lead, the dust and the need to keep my head down, I could not really look round to see how they were fixed. Maybe some had been hit or killed. The noise of enemy fire was unrelenting. The barrage of bullets seemed to intensify. I had no option. I started to crawl forward. And suddenly there they were, the Taliban, in my gunsight, firing from small buildings about 200 m directly to my front.

I fired off a couple of rounds to let them know we meant business. Then I looked to the left and right. Rabin and Dipendra were still glued to the ground, heads in the dust. Glancing back I saw that the rest of the section were also still in the open, completely exposed.

I was worried above all for my scouts. 'Rabin,' I yelled.

And again, 'Rabin, Rabin!' No answer or movement.

'Dipendra!' No response from him either.

The bullets smacked down, sending up plumes of sand and dirt all around us. I twisted round and shouted at the bhaiharu behind me. No reaction. In the noise of battle, how could anyone hear me?

The situation seemed impossible. Whichever way I went I would eventually be hit. I started to crawl to the rear, then changed my mind, twisted back and decided to go forward. As I tried to haul myself over the earth I felt my right foot sticking. It was snagged on some sort of obstruction. It felt like it was being pulled back.

I tried to carry on but the foot was going nowhere. I banged it on the ground in frustration. Then I risked a look round. What the …? There was Dipendra, still head down, now arms outstretched, holding on to my right boot for dear life. Trying to stop me getting killed. I could not help laughing. And, of course, I felt a surge of relief that he was alive.

But the situation was worse than ever. I screamed at him to let go of me and banged my right foot on the ground till he did so. Then I edged forward, trying to make my body as small as possible. To my right was the compound wall, and I noticed that a section of it was made not of mud and rock but of dry corn and grass. It looked flimsy enough for me to force my way through. On the other side of the wall I would be out of the direct line of fire.

So I crawled along the base of the wall to what looked like a weak point, stood up and kicked at the wall as hard as I could. It held. In desperation I started to headbutt it, hoping my helmet would smash open a hole. No effect. I tried with the butt of the rifle. Nothing. Dust was everywhere, except in my eyes, which were protected by goggles. I had been standing up all this time. Now I knelt, trying to make myself less of a target but aware I was still badly exposed.

At this point I spotted a pick-up truck 150 m ahead. Some of the Taliban had retreated inside it. There was a heavy machine gun mounted on the back. One of the fighters took aim and opened up on me and my brothers. I fired back and definitely hit the pick-up, but it was impossible to tell whether I had inflicted casualties.

I stood up and ran towards it, firing, shouting to Dipendra and Rabin to join me. The pick-up moved off, presenting a more difficult target. Inside, and from the heavy machine gun on the back, they continued firing on us.

Aiming accurately while upright and moving forward is not easy, but I did my best. I reached the end of the compound wall and found a ditch that offered good cover. Next to the ditch was a road, and beyond that an agricultural water channel, at least 20 m wide and who knew how deep? The enemy had chosen the ambush site well – the water channel presented a considerable obstacle and prevented us chasing after them.

Down in the ditch I settled into a good position and returned fire more effectively. The pick-up had disappeared by now. I was engaging men straight ahead of me, at a distance of 120 m. Then welcome voices: 'Guruji! Guruji!' Rabin and

Dipendra leapt into the ditch beside me. It was a great boost knowing they were unharmed, by my side. But I had no idea what had happened to the rest of my section, who the last I knew were pinned down without cover in the middle of that T-junction.

'OK, bhaiharu, listen up,' I shouted above the gunfire. 'Enemy are on the bund-line [any wall, ridge or tree-line that provides obvious cover] about one hundred and twenty metres directly in front. See them?'

'Seen, guruji.'

'OK. Rapid fire. *Rapid fire.*'

We put down rounds as fast as we could and I felt the balance begin to shift. We were giving as good as we got. And things were about to get better. A message on my PRR: 'We're on our way.' Not the cavalry but just as good. It was my 2IC, LCpl Dik. Thank God. The rest of my bhaiharu were good too.

'2IC, 2IC, wait out!' I instructed. We needed to put up a blizzard of covering fire before they joined us in the ditch. There's a simple logic to this: unless you hit the enemy hard, with everything you've got, they will retain the advantage and your chance of taking a fatal bullet remains high. We needed to get to the point where our fire was so relentless and accurate the enemy's priority would switch to saving their own lives, not trying to take ours.

So, as Dik and the rest of the section held back, we loaded fresh magazines into our rifles. Incoming fire continued to thud into the sandy lip of the ditch in front of us. '2IC, prepare to move,' I told Dik on the PRR.

Then, to Rabin and Dipendra: 'Bhaiharu! Rapid fire!'

Back on the PRR to Dik: 'Move now! *Move now!*'

The rest of the section piled into the ditch with us – every single one alive and well – and took over. The relief was immense. I still have no idea how Dipendra, Rubin and I survived the onslaught starting at the T-junction. The enemy rounds coming at us were heavy and well aimed, but missed. Perhaps it was due to our drill, our discipline, following SOPs and a refusal to panic. Or maybe it was just a case of God being on our side when it mattered.

At any rate, the full section was now assembled and on the offensive. And we had some pretty handy hardware – besides our individual weapons, two LMGs (light machine-guns), a GPMG (general purpose machine gun) and two LSWs (light support weapons). The enemy's weapons were no match for this degree of firepower. As our tracer rounds pinpointed the insurgents' positions, a calm professionalism settled over us in the ditch. This was like ambush or range training back in the UK.

My assumption was that if we did not kill them, the enemy would run and hide. But one of them, to his credit, held his ground and fired back. Maybe he did not know which way to run and decided to fight to the death. The rest retreated into the buildings behind them. In the heat of battle I cursed them as cowards but who could blame them, really, when confronted by some of the finest and bravest fighters on the planet!

We were calling the shots now. The battle was under our control. I admired the coolness of my brothers as, with the bullets flying around them, they took time to 'battle-clean' and oil their rifles, using a preparation made up back at base and put in small plastic bottles with holes in the lid. It's this kind of attention to detail that can save a life by ensuring that a weapon does not fail at a crucial moment.

The fighting continued. On the PRR I gave an assessment of the situation to my Platoon Commander, Lt Crawley, who was moving up behind us with the rest of the company. Then Bipen spotted an insurgent in open ground. Dipendra confirmed that he was running away. This was the frustrating thing. We desperately wanted to pursue and capture the enemy, but that irrigation channel (the water, we had worked out by now, was probably deep enough to drown in – especially with the loads we had) was blocking our way. If only we could reach the open ground beyond.

Trying to figure this out, I was overcome with exhaustion. It was all I could do to quench my thirst from my Camel-Bak hydration pack. Then, behind me, another potential game-changer – the Jackal patrol vehicles that had been sent forward by the OC had arrived, braking hard and stopping on the T-junction, just 5 m from where we were.

This was a huge morale-booster at a critical point in the battle. Their heavy weaponry – GPMG, .50-calibre guns and a GMG grenade launcher – joined the firepower of my bhai-haru in the ditch, increasing the noise of battle to earsplitting levels. I just about heard Dik, who was controlling and distributing the ammunition among our brothers, when he yelled: 'Ammo! Ammo! Ammo!'

I raised my head and rose on one knee to get a better view of the enemy. As I did so I heard a familiar and chilling sound. 'RPG, RPG!' I dived back down for cover, willing myself to shrink to as small a target as possible. At night it is easy to spot an incoming RPG as they generate a red-hot heat that is clearly visible. By day it is trickier, but by now I had had enough combat experience to recognize the sound and incoming smoke trail.

'RPG, RPG!' The brothers around me took up the cry, making sure that in the deafening levels of noise everyone knew what was about to hit. Then the ground shook. We were covered in dust and debris. I was not sure at first if we had been hit. I had faced RPGs many times in my military career, but this impact sounded different and was probably an airburst shell, designed to explode in the air and scatter lethal shards of metal. Thank God, a near miss. It had exploded on the top of the compound wall.

'Everyone all right?' I shouted. Everyone was good. But angry. That RPG had come seriously close. A bit lower and it could have wiped us all out. In response we laid down such a massive blitz of rounds on the enemy positions that the barrels of our weapons grew red-hot and we actually had to change the barrels on the GPMG and Minimi machine guns.

Meanwhile, behind us, Jackals were also blasting away with their vehicle-mounted heavy machine guns whilst moving up and down, presenting a more difficult target in the event of an RPG attack. As I looked back at them I heard screaming, then swearing: 'Shit, shit, shit ...'

A guy on top of one of the Jackals clutched at his shoulder and dropped. He had been hit (impossible to tell how badly), but the driver and commander at the front of the vehicle did not realize and kept firing.

I got on the PRR to inform the Platoon Commander and told those around me there was a casualty in one of the Jackals. Then I tried to get his attention. 'Hello mate, hello mate!' No reply, just the rattling sounds of the enemy's bullets all around. Despite the danger I jumped from the ditch and ran to the side of the vehicle, which was now stationary.

The casualty was nowhere to be seen. 'You OK, mate?' Nothing. I banged the side of the Jackal. 'You alright?' I moved to the back and found him by the rear door, holding his shoulder. Then I ran to the front and told his commander, who immediately threw the Jackal into reverse to escape the danger zone. At that point my Platoon Sergeant Shreeman Limbu and a medic showed up to extract the casualty. He was screaming. It did not sound good.

There was no let-up in the battle. This was one of the most dangerous fire fights I had ever been caught in and it had already been going for forty-five minutes. We were exhausted. Thirsty. Our ammo was low and so was our water. 'Happy birthday!' I said to myself. Would it end with me in a wooden box?

The prospect of dying did not frighten me. I had fought in some of the deadliest engagements of one of the most brutal conflicts of the twenty-first century – so far with barely a scratch to show for it. If my number was up now, on this dusty, lonely road, I could not really complain. My head was dropping, and then I thought of my family. My *two* families – my wife and children in the UK, my parents and relatives in Nepal.

If I took a bullet now there would be no more conversations with my children or my dear wife. No more being called 'son' by my mother and father. How would they survive without my support? The instinct for survival is a powerful one. Thoughts of home raised my fighting spirits. It was a no-brainer. I needed to get through this. I needed to kill the enemy before the enemy killed me.

As I took my binoculars from the top of my patrol pack the PRR crackled and a message from the OC, Maj Davies, came through to all C/S (Call Signs): 'Head down, head down. Air assist inbound, enemy position in figure, two minutes. Out.'

Saved by the bell. I told my bhaiharu a fighter plane was on its way. This was fantastic news – so long as it did not drop its missiles on us because we were so close to the enemy lines. Head down I squinted at my watch, counting down the two minutes. *Four, three, two, one* …. an earsplitting bang. A flash of silver in the blue and the plane disappeared over the horizon. Then the ditch was shaking, black smoke everywhere. Choking sounds as we spluttered in the smoke.

The smoke seemed to take forever to disperse. But when it did the picture was different. The air-dropped munition had changed the battle's momentum. The enemy were destroyed, they had been killed or stopped fighting and disappeared. We moved forward through their positions, while another platoon cleared the ground on the northern side as far as our stated Limit of Exploitation.

As day turns to evening in the desert the heat fades and cold sets in surprisingly quickly. At the end of battle my water bottle was empty. I was exhausted and parched and sweat poured from my forehead. A couple of hours later I was back in our makeshift camp in no man's land, surrounded by empty desert. We had eaten and quenched our thirst, dug shell scrapes, shared our rations and our experiences, sentries had been sent out to keep guard and I was huddled down, trying to keep warm.

What a day it had been. A day I knew I was lucky to see the end of. My birthday. And Alisa's. My thoughts turned to my daughter, the celebrations back in Folkestone. I pictured her lovely smile and remembered the small details that mean so much – how, whenever I went shopping in the local Tesco store, she would ask me to bring her something back and be waiting expectantly on my return.

It was a clear night, that night in no man's land in the desert. I lay on my back gazing at the Milky Way. There was a delicious breeze on my cheeks. The brilliant stars and distant sounds of cattle triggered memories. War and killing suddenly seemed far away, my simple village childhood within touching distance.

CHAPTER 3

STORM ON THE MOUNTAIN

It was a morning in the rainy season. I was nine years old, and I was about to set off with my father to walk to the house of my great uncle further down the valley. It had been raining heavily all night and we did not have any proper protection or umbrellas, so my dad was making some raincoats out of plastic sheeting. These would cover just our shoulders so our heads would get wet, but they were better than nothing.

As he folded the plastic I watched him. The picture of the two of us in our simple house told a story. He was sitting in a wooden chair that he had made himself. I was wearing a shirt that my mother had made from an old pair of my dad's trousers.

It was not exactly stylish, that shirt, but it lasted forever. That was how we lived, mending and making do.

I had been so excited, that morning, when Dad had asked if I wanted to go and visit my *tumba* (i.e. 'great uncle' in Gorkhali).

'Yes, please! Of course, *babu*!' (meaning 'father').

Tumba lived about 8 km down the valley. To get there we followed the path towards the Tawa River, which ran near his house. I loved going there as I got to play with my cousins and eat delicious food cooked by my great aunt – especially corn in buffalo milk.

It was hardly a dangerous journey but, as soon as we got there, we would always say the traditional prayer of thanks for arriving safely. It was also usual to sacrifice an animal as a gesture of thanks to God, who would then bestow good luck on our entire family. I was not so comfortable with this tradition. Would God really feel like blessing us after we had killed something that was alive? In my opinion a better way of making God feel happy and grateful was to love animals – to love all nature, not destroy it.

Maybe I was too soft. One of my jobs was to look after the family's chickens and goats, but when we were away from the house foxes would sometimes kill them. This made me so mad that one day I decided to make a trap – a box with food in one corner and a trap door so the fox could not get out once he had got in. It worked first time and I caught a small fox, maybe a cub. I had planned to kill it but as soon as I saw how beautiful it was, and how frightened, I just let it go. Twenty-five years on, I am pleased to say that attitudes to an animal sacrifice in the small villages of the Himalayas are changing. We usually offer up flowers instead.

Back to that rainy day in my childhood: my father handed me the plastic 'raincoat' as I took off that old shirt and put on some smart new clothes so I would look my best for my tumba and cousins. The clothes came from the market in the nearest big town – Taplejung or Gopetar – where we went once a year to buy things we could not get in Khebang.

My parents would bring back material, which they then had made up into different items of clothing by a tailor in the village. This was another tradition that made me uncomfortable at the time and more so when I think of it now. The local tailors were from a lower caste than us and therefore not allowed inside the house. They would have to work outside and we would bring them food as they sewed up our new clothes. And we would always wash the plate thoroughly before taking it back inside. To someone of my generation this strikes me now as really rude and prejudicial.

Full of excitement at the thought of visiting my great uncle, I was getting dressed as fast as I could in case my father left me behind or changed his mind. 'And wear your new shoes,' he said. These shoes were my pride and joy. My parents had given them to me the previous autumn on the festival of Dashain, one of the most important Hindu festivals in Nepal (think of it as Christmas and then some). It falls in September or October, running through *shukla pasha* (the fortnight when the moon is waxing) and ending at *poornima* (full moon).

At that time people returned from faraway to be with their families in their ancestral homes. The idea of the festival is to honour the goddess Durga, who symbolizes goodness and power, and her battle with the forces of evil.On the tenth day of the festival she finally triumphs over evil and this is when we receive *tika*, the distinctive red spot on the forehead made from a mixture of yoghurt, rice and vermilion, and the yellow mark made from *jamara*, i.e. barley seeds. The elders of the village bless us, and everyone has lots of fun dressing up in new clothes, joining processions and flying kites as well as (I'm afraid to say) sacrificing animals.

As part of these celebrations the year before, my parents had given me the smart shoes. After I had worn them for Dashain they were put away in a safe place until there was a special reason to wear them. And that was today. Then Mum tried to ruin everything, as mums sometimes do, by being far too sensible. 'Kailash,' she said, 'just look at that rain. I do not think it is a good idea for you to go. The way down will be slippery and dangerous.'

I knew she was saying this for the right reasons. She always did. She loved me as only a mother can and always had my best interests at heart. And she did have a point about the rain which, far from showing any sign of stopping, was now coming down more heavily than ever.

She knew that the rain would make the path treacherous. The route down the valley followed a hillside and rice paddies on one side, with a stream on the other. Rocks and boulders lined the edges of the rice fields, which were sodden with rain.

And the rain could trigger a mudslide on the hill that would sweep down through the rice paddies, catching the boulders – and us – in its flow.

'Oh, *muuuum!*' I whined. 'Please let us go! *Pleeeeeease!*' I begged her with all my heart. There had been lots of times when she had decided it was just too dangerous for me to go out. I was determined she would not get her way on this occasion. Like all children, I knew how to get round my parents. My strategy was basically just to go on *and on* till she caved in.

Eventually it worked. She sighed and gave us her blessing, making us promise to take the utmost care and to turn back at the first sign of trouble. Dad, meanwhile, had been waiting impatiently outside the house, anxious to get going. 'We're running really late, son,' he called. 'Remember, we've got to get back home before darkness falls. The path will be ready dangerous in the dark.'

'OK, babu. Coming!'

I was so happy in those moments. Full of energy, jumping with joy at the thought of playing with my cousins and eating scrumptious food. The journey to my great uncle's house really was not so far, I told myself. I felt as if I was flying and actually started to run and jump along the path in front of my father.

'Kailash, slow down! You'll have a nasty accident.'

'Sorry, babu.'

Soon enough the path became very slippery and treacherous, and then I did not feel quite so joyful. My precious new shoes were already all but ruined by the mud and rain. I had been looking forward to showing them off to my cousins. Now I worried about how scruffy they would look. And then the leeches started to attack me. Those disgusting blood-sucking worms are the worst creatures in the world. Westerners think that just because they are common in the wet forests where we live, we are used to them and do not think they are so bad. Let me assure you that we Nepalis hate them as much as you!

Of course, the rainy season brings them out in their thousands. They just sit and wait in the oozing ground until some juicy flesh walks by. That morning I soon felt them latching on to my legs, getting into my shoes. They especially like small cuts in your skin that they can get their horrible teeth into. I felt them feasting on one of my cold big toes, but there's nothing you can do but try to ignore them.

Incidentally, if you want a tip for getting rid of them: do not, whatever you do, just pull them off – the whole mouth and sucking mechanism is likely to stay embedded in your flesh! And the way they show you in old films, burning them with the end of a lit cigarette, does not work. Just wait a few minutes till they have drunk their fill, and they will drop off of their own accord, or you can rub salt on them with a rag. Then flick them well away, clean the wound and put some antiseptic on it. That's Dr Kailash's advice!

But back to that day. We soldiered on, my father and I. The rain was falling more heavily than ever, the 'raincoat' that Dad had given me didn't really work and the terrain was getting harder and harder to walk on. I did my best to ignore the leeches and the general discomfort and think of all the fun I would have . . . but at the same time we really had to concentrate on where we were putting our feet.

We had both been out before in such conditions, my father probably a hundred times. We both knew that one slip and we could be killed or badly injured. And there were no medics to help us, no hospital nearby where we could be treated. The best we could hope for was that one of the village shamans or medicine men would come out. Or a local. Living so remotely, quite a few villagers had to have a basic knowledge of first aid; my grandfather taught me what to do if a snake bit me but, thankfully, I never had to put it to the test.

The going was tough and slow, but we navigated what we thought were the worst sections of the path and eventually got to within half a mile of tumba's house. At this point I relaxed and started to feel excited again. Soon I would be playing volleyball with my cousins, working up an appetite for all those plates of delicious food.

Then, out of nowhere, came a terrible sound, a sound so loud, so terrifying, so different to anything I had ever heard – including the loudest thunderclap – that I froze to the spot and stared all round at the trees, looking for an explanation. Then again. And then a different noise, as if someone was screaming in pain. Had the ground moved? I looked down at the sodden earth, feeling suddenly unsteady on my feet.

'Babu, babu!' I shouted for my dad, who was about 20 m ahead on the path, and ran to him. He held me. 'What's happening?' I said.

He did not need to say anything. It was soon obvious. The

earth really was shaking. The terrible sounds seemed to be coming from the rocks that bordered the path to one side and above us. Higher still, the whole tree-line was trembling. My father yelled louder than I had ever heard him yell. 'Oh no! Mudslide coming!'

I screamed. I remember thinking, *these are the last moments of my life*. The slide started with a shower of small stones smacking down from the surrounding hills. My father had recovered his wits and was trying to move us along the path and out of harm's way. Some hope. We crouched along, trying to dodge the bigger stones. Then the ground shook again and this time it was more violent and even louder than before, like an earthquake.

This terrified me so much that I stopped in my tracks as if had been turned to rock. I froze. Then I witnessed something unbelievable and amazing. The earth was actually moving. Above us the hillside was shifting, sliding down, carrying trees and boulders with it. Coming straight for us.

What I remember, more than anything, is the reaction of the birds and animals. The air was suddenly alive with flapping wings and alarm calls. You would think all the birds had to do was keep airborne but not all of them made it. I saw one fall into the moving mud, struggle to get out, get sucked under. A white feather was all that was left.

As for the animals – I saw a sight that still haunts me. Encrusted like jewels in this churning brown mass were goats and buffaloes, bellowing in fear as the air was squeezed out of them. Maybe it is not right to say that animals think and feel exactly like us, but in those moments they were no different. For me it was as if Nature herself was sobbing and my heart broke for all the animals that were dying in agony around us.

My father had thoughts only for us, and how the hell we were going to survive. Clods of earth and stones were battering us. We could cope with that but worse, much worse, was on its way. Up on the tree-line a huge boulder was starting to work loose. And that mudslide continued to rumble towards us. Dad gripped my hand and we started to run as best we could. We were now probably over 300 m from my great uncle's house. We had to get there before the mudslide engulfed us.

At one point, as we ran, I saw a cow bellowing in agony being crushed between two moving boulders. I tugged at my dad's arm, begging him to stop and help. He yanked me forward, saying, 'Do you want to die as well?' I closed my eyes. The tears were streaming down my face as we stumbled on. I said a silent prayer: *Please God, save us.*

The wind was howling. The birds and animals were crying. The earth itself was calling out in anguish. And then, more rumbling, louder than thunder, and the ground beneath our feet trembled again. The mudslide was doubling in energy. We had no chance of beating it. Any minute we were going to be sucked under.

My father made a snap decision. If we continued forward it would be certain death. Our only hope was to retrace our steps. He swung me round and we started back the way we had come. I trusted him to know what was best. And the feel of him squeezing my hand was reassuring. My heart was pumping.

I was breathing rapidly. 'Try not to panic,' he said.

Easier said than done. I was scared to death. I could not help glancing up at the mudslide, the way it seemed on a collision course to bury us. Would it stop before it reached us? Could we outrun it? The path was so flooded that we were making slower and slower progress. My dad made another decision, to abandon the path and try to find an escape route through the sodden rice paddies. Yet this slowed us down even more.

Three steps in, my foot stuck fast. One of my new shoes was locked in the deep mud. Whichever direction we took, the mudslide seemed to follow us. Now it was right here in the rice paddies. All around us, the precious crop of the village was being destroyed. The mudslide kept on coming.

My father tugged my arm. 'Hurry!' he shouted. But I was exhausted. The more I tried to move, the more I felt my feet sinking into the bottomless mud. He was trying to pull me out but his fingers were slipping from mine. This was my worst moment. I really felt I had reached the point of no return. I thought of all that was dearest to me – my mother, my dog Denney, the pig, the goats, the cows. I would never see them again.

I was sinking lower. The mud was squeezing me tighter. I wondered about the moment of death. There was not so much pain so far. What would it take to kill me? Would it hurt? And the 'journey' after that? Would I wake up in another world?

'Please, Dad!' I pleaded with my father to do *something*. But he was in his own hell. Our fingers had now broken apart. His eyes looked into mine with infinite tenderness. I knew he would do anything – sacrifice his life – to save me. But I also knew he was powerless. He was sinking into the mud. And the more he struggled, the deeper he sank.

The suffering was etched on his face. I could not look at him. I closed my eyes and prayed to God to save us. Now I was half-floating and half-submerged in the watery mud. Then I heard his voice and thought I must be imagining it: 'Kailash! Quick!'

The pain from the mud squeezing my body was excruciating. It was all I could do to whisper back, 'OK, babu.' I opened my eyes and saw that my father was still very much alive. He had found a second wind from somewhere and was straining afresh to get out of the mud. I was still powerless. I could not move. Could not help him. All I could do was bear witness to his life-and-death struggle.

Rocks and stones kept flying through the air and the mud was piling up, thickening around me. It reached my chin. Then a miracle – my father was free. His limbs were moving. I could see his legs and arms moving towards me. Then my head was under the mud, I was drowning *in mud*. I remember feeling bitter and angry, that God would not keep me alive for long enough for my father to save me.

No breath left. Sinking. Hopeless. My father's voice again, as if in a dream. 'Kailash! Don't worry – I've got you.' His hands under my arms, tugging. But my body was not moving. Not one inch. There was nothing I could do to help. I was trapped, there in the wind and rain, with the anguished cries of frightened birds and dying animals all around, and decided that he was never going to get me out. The best thing for Dad was to save himself.

Probably he knew that too but he could not leave me. Hopelessly, he cried out, 'Help, help! Somebody *please* help us!' As if anybody else would be nearby in that nightmare of mud and rain. As if, even if they were, they could have heard him above the terrible noise.

But he never gave up trying to save me. 'Push,' he said, 'push against the ground.'

When I opened my mouth to reply it filled with mud. I pushed. He pulled. Then a boulder was coming towards us. I saw its shape, blotting out the light. Heard its terrible rumble. Closed my eyes and prayed as hard as I have ever prayed to the hill goddess Pathibara Devi.

Somewhere, out there on that broken mountain, Pathibara took pity on us. The boulder did not crush us but rolled on down the valley. And my body was suddenly feeling lighter. My lungs were filling with air. My father was lifting me free of the mud and I was spluttering and yelling like a newborn baby. At the moment of death I had been born anew.

I sobbed my thanks and my father hugged me to him. But there was no time to be lost. The nightmare was not over. We had to get ourselves to safety, to a part of the mountain where the mud was not sliding. My father grabbed my hand. My feet were numb and not responding. He dragged me through the mud.

We had barely made 10 m when the rice paddy in front of us was swept up by a wave of mud and trees. We watched in disbelief as it disappeared down the mountain. At that moment we found our escape route – a ridge of solid earth. We ran and fell and got back up, and clawed our way along it. And slowly the noise and the danger subsided until Dad judged it safe enough for us to stop. I collapsed on the ground. Exhausted. Still terrified. Sobbing. My whole body shaking. Unable to get any words out. Not even 'Thank you'.

My father held me in his arms. 'You're safe now.'

This terrible episode was a lesson for me in parental love. My mother had carried me for nine months, giving me life through every cell of her body. My father had just risked his life to save mine. They would starve to give me food. Freeze on the open mountain to give me shelter. Some people travel the world seeking the kindness and mercy of God. But you do not have to go that far. You just have to look up into the eyes of your mother and father.

We never made it to my great uncle's house that day. We hurried back home through the rain and got there just as it was getting dark. Mum was waiting anxiously and could not believe it when she saw the state we were both in. Me especially – my new clothes in shreds, the precious shoes broken beyond repair. Dad tried to play down what had happened, but she was not stupid. She did not need to say anything, the look in her eyes said it all: 'I was right, you see. Your mother always knows best.'

I was nine years old and this was my first brush with death. It would be far from my last.

CHAPTER 4

CONTACT AT
MUSA QALA

Here's what you get when you stick eight exhausted soldiers in a 4 m × 4 m tent and switch the light off: snoring so loud it sounds like a herd of buffaloes with toothache. To be honest I was the worst snorer of the lot – but there were no snores coming from me that night. I was as knackered as the rest of them but just could not get off to sleep. It was the summer of 2006, 0100 hours, Camp Bastion, Helmand Province, Afghanistan.

Over the years Camp Bastion grew from nothing; from just a few tents in the desert to a 'town' for more than 20,000 personnel and a landing strip capable of taking Boeing C17 transport planes. In spring 2006, when we arrived with 3 Para (3rd Battalion, the Parachute Regiment) as part of the Operation known as 'Herrick IV', it was just getting going. Much of it was still a building site, everything was covered in dust from the frequent sandstorms and accommodation was in tents with no air conditioning, despite sweltering night-time temperatures.

The task of 3 Para was to maintain a security zone in northern Helmand. It soon became clear that many places harboured Taliban sympathizers, and it was decided to deploy small, fortified bases in various districts to stop them being overrun by insurgents. Our job, the following morning, was to provide protection on a resupply mission to the base at Musa Qala. The Taliban had besieged the base for several weeks and the lads inside badly needed fresh supplies of water, fresh fruit and vegetables, ammunition and spare parts.

So brutal was the Taliban stranglehold that at that precise moment Musa Qala was one of the most dangerous places on the planet. As I lay in my 'cot' bed, listening to the snoring of my fellow Gurkhas, I heard an explosion in the distance and wondered what the day would have in store.

It was only about 96 km from Camp Bastion to Musa Qala. I say 'only' but the route lay across empty desert, through rocky wadis (valleys) and drifts of sand. We were travelling in a convoy of supply vehicles, with us in WMIKs (Weapons Mount Installation Kit; basically, a soft-skinned Land Rover with machine guns mounted on the back) providing the firepower and protection.

It took the convoy of about a dozen vehicles the whole of one day and the early morning of the next to reach the outskirts of Musa Qala. At 0800 hours, as we approached the town, my WMIK got stuck in the deep sand; the engine was revving but the gears were not engaging and suddenly we were going nowhere fast. Not a good place for this to happen. We were slightly off the top of a small ridge of sand and stone, on a fairly steep slope and in the direct line of fire from insurgent positions. I was particularly worried for Rfn Gajbahadur Gurung (known as 'Gaj'), who was manning the machine gun – a big, heavy, .50 cal automatic weapon with a range of over 1.6 km – up top.

'Reverse the vehicle!' I instructed the driver, Rfn Ambika.

'OK, guruji.'

He crunched the gears. The engine groaned. Nothing happened. Maybe the vehicle had taken a hit, or we had damaged it crossing the rough desert. Then the Taliban guns opened up. We felt the rattling of bullets skimming our heads.

In those situations you expect to be shot at any second. You're just waiting for that one bullet. At one point, sitting in the stationary WMIK, I suddenly felt excruciating pain in my upper body and thought I had been hit. I checked for signs of blood, feeling the small gaps between the plates of body armour.

A story one of my gurujis once told me came to mind. A gun battle was raging. Several of our men were hit at the same time but, for the first few moments, none of them realized or felt the pain. They carried on fighting. Then they began to drop. They knew they were dying and they held on to one another for a final farewell. I still was not sure whether I had been hit or not.

I could not find any blood. But that did not necessarily mean anything.

There was no let-up in the enemy barrage. The bullets struck seconds apart. The pain in my side grew worse. I was worried about my brother in the most exposed position of all, on the machine gun. Gaj was one of the bravest and brightest men in my section. So far he had not fired back.

I shouted as loud as I could above the rattle of incoming gunfire: 'Gaj! You OK?' No reply. Bullets kept bursting. 'Gaj, Gaj! Can you hear me? You OK up the top there?'

The sounds of battle were so loud – like the worst gale blowing over our heads – that maybe he just could not hear me and he was fine. On the other hand, if he had been hit would I have heard his screams? He could already be dead and about to fall off the WMIK. The fact that he had not returned fire was seriously worrying.

Just behind us on the ridge and further back on the road to Musa Qala, the rest of the convoy was also pinned down by enemy fire. It appeared to be coming from a position below the ridge, about 300 m away in the direction of the town. As I was trying to identify the exact spot Ambika, in the driving seat, got very worked up. 'What's happening with the vehicle?' he shouted.

It was starting to slide down the slope. At the bottom was a deep ditch. We were heading for disaster. I was worried as hell, but a leader needs to project a cool exterior. Making good decisions in war depends upon keeping calm. 'OK,' I said, 'let's sort this out. Slowly does it.'

I also had Gaj to think about. As the WMIK continued to slide I called his name again, but no response. Risking making more of a target of myself I half-stood and twisted my head to get a better view of the back of the vehicle. Gaj was still there and appeared to be holding the gun, but it was impossible to see if he was OK.

There was no alternative. However dangerous it was I needed to get out of the vehicle – see if Gaj needed help, see if I could stop the WMIK sliding down the ridge. 'Hang on, Ambika!' I grabbed my rifle and jumped. I underestimated the gradient and when I landed almost fell over and rolled down the slope.

As I was steadying myself on the sand I heard Gaj shouting from the back of the WMIK, 'Guruji! Engaging enemy!' He was OK after all. I had no way of knowing why he had not answered my shouts before. Or had not been returning fire. Maybe he had been concentrating on getting a precise sighting of the enemy and had wanted to save ammunition until he could make it count.

One thing was certain. Nobody was more anxious than Gaj to teach the Taliban a lesson. Several mates of his from the section had been badly injured by enemy fire and he was desperate to pay them back.

As Gaj got ready to open fire with his machine gun I went round to the front of the WMIK and tried to stop it sliding. Behind the wheel Ambika was still 'gunning' the engine, trying to engage reverse gear. Leaning against the vehicle I pushed with all my strength but it made no difference. The

WMIK continued to slide slowly downward. The problem was that, with the combined weight of the machine gun and the machine gunner, it was seriously top-heavy. Then Gaj opened up with the .50 cal.

'Enemy, enemy!' he shouted. Then an earsplitting noise. The recoil shook the WMIK like a piece of rag and I thought for a moment it was going to slide out of control down the slope. 'They're running away!' Gaj said. But he was being optimistic. The incoming fire continued, now from multiple locations. I knew we had to take drastic action.

'Gaj, jump out.'

'OK, guruji.' He landed beside me and we took cover as best we could by the side of the WMIK. 'What's going on?' he said into my ear as the bullets peppered us. He was so hyped up he did not seem to have noticed the vehicle was rolling slowly down the slope. Now he put his weight next to mine and we tried to halt the slide. Not a chance.

I feared the worst. There was nothing we could do to stop the WMIK hitting the bottom of the slope and tipping into the ditch. Always, in my pocket, I keep a 'lucky coin' my mother gave me to protect me in moments of danger. It has a hole in the middle and Mum wound it tightly with white thread and attached a green-and-white lanyard. She gave it to me in 2002, on my first trip home to Nepal after I had joined the Gurkhas. It has never been out of my possession since. I squeezed it hard in my fist.

I reckoned that if the vehicle did roll into the ditch Gaj and I would be OK, we could move away and find cover in the rough terrain. But the driver, Ambika, would be caught like a fly in a trap. He would stand no chance. Not with that incoming fire.

And then, when all seemed lost, the front tyres were picking up a little traction – just enough to help us stop it sliding. I thanked my lucky coin, I thanked my mother. Gaj jumped back up behind his .50. I returned to my seat where my gun, a GPMG (General Purpose Machine Gun), was mounted in front of the commanders' section of the WMIK.

Bullets were flying in all directions. I looked back. About 48 m away, three of our WMIKs had lined up and opened fire on the Taliban. This gave me and my brothers vital cover. And it bought me time to pinpoint the exact location of the enemy through my binoculars.

It was not enough to know the general direction they were firing from. If I could find the precise spot, the GPMG could take them all out. There was no point wasting ammunition by firing indiscriminately.

Meanwhile, I could see that half a dozen of our resupply trucks were slowly approaching Musa Qala, taking the vital provisions for the FOB that had been under siege there for so long. It must have been a welcome sight. The men, also worn down by heavy fighting, were getting a bit desperate.

The enemy were making life as difficult as possible. They were obviously well prepared to attack this resupply mission. They had probably been lying in wait for days or even weeks, and knew exactly what to do. The firefight intensified as they targeted not just us, but the supply vehicles entering Musa

Qala. The relentless barrage of noise reminded me of some-thing – the fireworks display on the River Thames in London, to celebrate the New Year!

The smoke trails told me that they were deploying RPGs as well as mortars and automatic weapons. The front of the WMIK had been hit but, by the grace of God, we were still safe – and we still had not fought back with the full force we had at our disposal.

This was because of the danger of accidentally hitting non-combatants. In *A Soldier's Guide to the Law of Armed Conflict* it states that 'care must be taken to avoid or minimize incidental loss or damage to civilians'. This was always a pri-ority when we fought the enemy in built-up areas. We were supposed to be protecting the Afghani people, not shooting them. But we were in a hole and needed to fight our way out of it with care and accuracy. However difficult the situation on the battlefield, the Gurkhas have never given up or run away. Our forefathers, I'm proud to say, won two VCs in the First World War and ten in the Second World War.

As the bullets and bombs raked us I instructed Ambika to turn the WMIK towards the enemy, so we could get a better view and a better arc of fire. Up top, Gaj was returning fire. He shouted down: 'Guruji! The enemy's run away. They're hiding inside the building.'

'OK,' I yelled back at him. 'Engage if you see them. En-sure safety of civilians.'

But the incoming fire continued. 'Bloody hell! Now they're firing non-stop rounds!' Standing up there, he had a great line of vision. But it also left him completely exposed. A sitting duck. Gaj was a brave man.

'Do you see them?' I asked.

'No yet, guruji. I'm looking.'

I continued to do the same with the binoculars from the front of the vehicle. From my combat experience I have learned just how tricky it can be to locate the enemy with any precision. Often we are fighting on difficult terrain with plenty of obstructions. If they are in buildings or behind compound walls you have to look out for dust, smoke, muzzle flash, the glint of light on the barrel of a weapon. You rely on the naked eye as well as binoculars. It requires skill, concentration and patience.

While we held our ground, the vehicles lined up behind us were returning a massive barrage of fire. I could see the tracer rounds striking the building that Gaj had already identified, where we suspected they were firing from. I studied the building through my binoculars. But it was hard to get a steady view as the WMIK continued to be rocked by incoming fire.

It looked likely to me that they were engaging from behind the compound walls next to the building. There were small holes in the walls, just big enough to take a rifle barrel. But I could not be sure. I could fire in this general direction but I did not want to waste ammunition; who knew what might happen later? It was also possible that without proper targeting I might hit civilians. Feeling frustrated I continued to look – with the naked eye now – for telltale signs of dust, smoke or sudden movement.

Then bingo – a man with a rifle appeared from behind the wall and moved fast to take cover behind the corner of the building. As I watched he started shooting at us. Instinctively I shouted, 'Enemy! Enemy!'

It was the moment I had been waiting for. I controlled the GPMG, brought it onto my shoulder, aimed and opened up with a long burst of fire – perhaps the longest continuous burst in my entire army career. It could be, in the course of the many firefights I have had in Afghanistan, that the bullets I fired killed and injured many enemy fighters. I have no way of knowing and I try not to think about it. I cannot afford to have regret or sadness. The fact is that I only pulled the trigger when I was fired on first, and it came down to kill or be killed. On this occasion I gave everything I had got but at the end of it the enemy was still standing, still shooting at us. I could hardly believe I had not hit him.

As I continued to fire the GPMG I instructed Gaj and Ambika: 'Listen in, bhaiharu; two hundred and fifty metres in our axis [i.e. directly in front] – compound alone, big house, right corner compound – enemy! Rapid fire!'

Gaj was on it. And Ambika opened up with his personal SA80 assault rifle.

'Where are the bastards again?' shouted Gaj.

I could not have been clearer: 'Tracer two hundred and fifty metres in our axis – small trees – right, three o'clock, building with compound – inside the compound, enemy!'

'I see him!'

All three of us were firing. I could see the dust kicking up but we kept missing.

'Kill the Taliban!' shouted Gaj.

The Taliban was still standing, still firing back. I have to give him his due. Maybe he wanted to show his colleagues how brave he was, but he did show a lot of courage in standing there in such an exposed position, taking us on. There were so many rounds coming in that I reckoned he was not alone, that there were other Taliban firing from inside the building.

Between the three of us on our WMIK and the other convoy vehicles further down the valley, we now had greater firepower than the enemy. This was a complete reversal of the balance of power around Musa Qala for the past few weeks. We had turned the tables.

The whole fighting arena was full of dust and noise. But the most important thing – the reason we were here and risking our lives every second – was that the 're-sup' vehicles were getting through. The FOB was being re-stocked with battle supplies and there was nothing the Taliban could do to stop it.

Gaj and Ambika kept up a running commentary as they poured lead into the enemy positions.

'He's running away, he's running away! Bloody hell! I'll kill you if you come back!'

'We'll kill you, bastard!'

Then I felt something hot on my neck. I screamed, '*Aatha! Aatha!*' (A general exclamation.) I felt my neck, trying to remove what was burning me.

'Guruji! You OK?' Ambika said.

I had no answer. I was too busy feeling my neck. Whatever it was I could not find or remove it. I began to panic. A bullet? I had never been shot – is this what it felt like? What was it?

I looked at my hands. No sign of blood.

I carried on firing and gradually the burning sensation began to fade. Then I found out what it was – an empty brass case from a 5.56 bullet that fell down into the footwell of the vehicle. The red-hot case had probably flipped from Ambika's rifle, stuck in my clothing and burned my neck!

With the binoculars I made another scan of the building and compound where the rest of the enemy were firing. Now that the one guy we had spotted had run away, it was back to square one. It was impossible to pinpoint their exact whereabouts. By this time our blood was up. We wanted to confront them face-to-face. Take them on in hand-to-hand combat.

To us in those moments they were cowards, hiding in deep holes, fighting like rats. We believe the ultimate weapon is the khukuri, the traditional Gurkha knife. We all grew up with them – almost, it felt, from birth. It was a tool, a symbol, a precious thing that we kept on us at all times. I knew that the two brothers under my command on the WMIK really wanted the chance to take the Taliban on with their khukuris. I felt the same. But we needed to stay calm, conserve ammunition, be patient.

Now I concentrated the binoculars on a series of small, one-storey mud-walled structures within the compound where I suspected the enemy may be hiding. As I was doing this something caught my eye. 'Bloody hell!' I yelled. I could see rifle barrels poking through the compound wall. Not one or two but several. Then a muzzle flashed as he fired on us. No wonder we could not see them. They were crouched out of sight behind the wall. And they were well protected. The wall may have been made of 'mud', but it was so thick and dense that our bullets could not penetrate it. And they had a clear sight of us.

This was so frustrating. I was desperate for one or more of them to move out into the open where we could get a clear sighting. My GPMG was ready on my shoulder and my index finger on the trigger. Then it happened. A figure suddenly appeared in the compound, running towards the main building. He was carrying a rifle and, as he reached the door of the building, he turned in our direction and fired.

'Enemy! Enemy!' I yelled. I aimed the GPMG and shot back. The weapon was loaded with tracer rounds – one in every four (known as 4-bit), then every other round (1-bit). The tracers ignite on firing so you can follow the trajectory and adjust for accuracy. And other shooters can use it to pinpoint the enemy. The flipside, of course, is that the enemy can use it to pinpoint *you*.

I followed my tracer bullets and they seemed to be landing right on top of the target. But he got away – disappeared through the door and into the building. More frustration and anger. With the adrenaline pumping all I wanted to do was charge into the house, grab him by the throat and tell him what I thought: 'You're a coward! If you were a man you'd come out and fight. You think you're brave? Then why are you hiding? If you're such a fearless warrior why do you plant IEDs? Come out and let's do this properly!'

These are the words that run through your head in the battlefield. But sometimes I had other thoughts. There were plenty of firefights when the enemy took heavy casualties. They died painful deaths. Perhaps they asked for water before closing their eyes for the last time. Or longed to see and hold their newborn child. They all had a family who loved them as ours loved us. They were human, too.

But that did not mean that we would ever ease up on the intensity of our fight against them. In whatever situation we found ourselves in, the message we always tried to put across was: 'We're Gurkhas. Don't you dare mess with us!'

And now I really wanted to push on for a face-to-face confrontation. On my PRR I called up the Platoon Commander, WO2 Trilochan Gurung, who was further down the valley behind us and requested permission to move forward. He denied it. Told us to stay where we were and engage the enemy from there.

The bullets were flying in both directions. Clouds of smoke and dust were coming off the top of the building and the compound walls.

'Enemy, enemy!' yelled Gaj and opened up again with his .50 cal. 'Bloody Taliban!' Then, 'Guruji! They're running away!'

'Rapid fire!' I shouted.

The enemy were actually being smart and strategic – remaining under cover, keeping us in their sights. We had to keep calm and be equally smart. All the yelling and swearing was just letting off steam. We had to shoot fast and accurately whenever we had a decent sighting; easier said than done in a firefight with all that noise and dust. But this is what we train for. At the same time we must stick to the ROE regarding civilian casualties, proportionate force and only firing on the enemy when attacked first. Even in the heat of battle, when our lives are on the line, we need to maintain control. This is how we remain effective as a fighting force. It is also how we minimize the likelihood of losing lives on our side.

It might sound like stating the obvious but the death of a soldier is a terrible thing. You lose your brother. You lose your friend. It really damages morale. And then the effects ripple outwards, to family and friends back in Nepal or the UK. You will do anything to stop it happening, but sometimes the odds are against you.

On this occasion I was amazed that we had not taken a hit with all the firepower coming at us. The advantage was definitely with the Taliban. They were protected by the wall – even the .50 cal would not penetrate it. And they had a clear shot at us. Our best bet for shifting them was air strikes or ILAW (Interim Lightweight Antitank Weapon – a shoulder-fired antitank missile).

Or tanks. And that was what happened now. I noticed sound and movement about 450 m behind us. 'Hey, Ambika!'

'Yes, guruji?'

'Look behind you. CVR.' (CVR, or CVRT, stands for Combat Vehicle Reconnaissance/Tracked, a small, highly manoeuvrable armoured vehicle with armour-piercing cannon.)

'Wow, guruji!'

A moment later the cannon opened up. It was a huge morale-booster. With the CVRT providing cover we could stop firing ourselves and concentrate on locating the enemy positions.

A few seconds later yet another new sound filled the air. I looked up. Two of our fighter jets, so high they were just flashes of silver. This was even more of a boost to our fighting spirit. I knew from experience that the enemy are more afraid of air attack than anything else. When they see planes they hide like rats. They were probably already scrambling to find the best shelter.

Their incoming fire slackened off, as expected. But we were still under attack, mainly from a sniper who was taking carefully aimed shots. Then the radio in the WMIK burst into life. I picked up the handset. It was the Platoon Commander: 'Air strike approaching.' Fighter jets were about to drop missiles on the enemy positions.

I told Ambika and Gaj and we just kept our heads down and waited. Then an update. 'Sixty seconds out.' Keeping my head down I looked at my watch, following the second hand tick down: twenty, ten, five …

Two earth-rocking explosions. I lifted my head, saw the planes swooping back up, disappearing as quickly as possible into the furthest corner of the sky. A moment later, flames shot 30 m plus from the building and compound where the enemy had been hiding. Then a great wall of smoke and dust. I tried to make out the impact points but the air was too thick. And Gaj was yelling, 'You bloody deserve it!'

As the smoke and dust dispersed I studied the site through my binoculars. The building had disappeared into a pile of smoking rubble. I reckoned there was not much chance any of the Taliban had survived that onslaught. Or if they had they would most likely be fatally injured or in severe shock. They would certainly have lost their hearing. I had frequently come across that. Perhaps they had also lost their minds. The terror, the noise, the awesome destructive power of the missiles would be enough to send anybody crazy. I imagined them closing their eyes, waiting for death.

There was now a lull. No firing, and a strange quiet, except for the ringing in my ears. I watched the building – or where the building had been – and the smashed compound through the binoculars, looking for signs of life, wondering if anybody would stumble forward making signs of surrender. No one did.

Then the planes came back. Just to make sure. The enemy position was pulverized with more missiles. More flames, dust and smoke. We were still standing by to fight the enemy if needed, but I reckoned I could now safely say that we were no longer targets. There was no one left with any fighting capability. No one at all.

A few minutes later the re-sup vehicles finished unloading the vital provisions into the FOB, and the convoy started to regroup before setting off on the return journey across the desert. The fighter planes continued to circle high above in case a surprise attack but, finally, we felt able to relax. I thanked God that we had accomplished our mission and for bringing us through such a dangerous battle with not a single casualty.

It was a long journey back to Camp Bastion. We made slow progress and, as the light began to fade, our Platoon Commander made the decision to stop and make camp in the desert for the night. We stopped in a spot surrounded by mountains. It was a beautiful place and I paused to watch as the sun sank between two peaks.

But we had work to do before complete darkness descended. We were at the end of a day of bloody warfare and the danger was still with us. Our first priority was to park all gun-mounted vehicles to face the points of an anticipated attack. Then we set about the post-battle routine of checking and cleaning weapons and equipment. Ambika carefully inspected the vehicles, checking tyres and refuelling them from jerry cans. We laid out ammunition, ready for use.

These activities are all standing operating procedures that are so important after any kind of battlefield operation, however tired, hungry, thirsty or sleep-deprived we may be. They take five to ten minutes and may save our lives if we are suddenly, unexpectedly attacked.

The mosquitoes were bad that night. We rigged up nets over the cot beds out in the open and that felt to me like luxury – I have been on plenty of operations near the enemy lines when I've had to sleep on the ground without a sleeping bag or mattress. I lay down for a quick rest, feeling very satisfied with a successful day and a job well done. My wife and children, back in the UK, came to mind; how much I looked forward to seeing them again.

Yet I could not sleep. My eyes were stinging with all the dust that covered my face. I sat up and tried to wash it off with a little of my drinking water. My mouth was dry, my lips felt numb. I drank a bottle of water and the three of us – Gaj,

Ambika and I – started to cook. The rest of the section were looking after themselves in another vehicle.

In our mess tins we heated up a 24-hour ration pack of noodles with some dry meat my wife had sent me and some chillis. We were starving and it smelled fantastic, it tasted good too. We ate sitting on our cots and drank more water, making sure there was still a full spare jerry can of drinking water in the WMIK. I was so tired.

A moment later I was back in bed. It was cold by then. I covered my head with the hood of the sleeping bag so just my face was exposed and lay there looking at the stars, feeling the fresh wind on my cheeks as I used to back in my mountain home in Nepal. In the distance dogs barked and donkeys brayed. I thought they sounded in pain. Then I fell asleep.

CHAPTER 5

AN EARLY LESSON

I was about ten years old and walking home from school with my friend Tej. The small village school was on the other side of a mountain ridge, a 30-minute walk from where we lived. We felt hungry because we always felt hungry on schooldays – they did not give us food there. But we felt good. The sun was shining. A breeze was blowing, gently rocking the trees. It was early afternoon. We had hours of time ahead of us. 'We don't have to go home yet,' I told Tej.

We decided to make a detour into the forest to look for fruit, some bananas and plums. We were not really allowed to go into the forest at that age as it was easy to get lost and you might meet dangerous wild animals. So the fruit idea was partly just an excuse to have a little adventure. But we did find some bananas and we gobbled them down.

When we finally got back to our village we were running a bit late. Tej's house was the first one we came to and, as we approached it, we saw that his uncle, who lived with them, was standing outside, waiting. When he spotted us he began to shout and scream at Tej, 'Where have you been? What have you been doing?'

I was so scared that I ran off and did not stop running till I had reached my house a few minutes later. My mum and dad did not seem to notice that I was late. I did not tell them where we had been and I did not mention Tej's angry uncle. Usually, once I had had something to eat at home I would go to Tej's house to play. But I was too scared to go that day. I thought his uncle might lose his temper with me as well.

The next morning I walked past his house on the way to school. Usually Tej would be waiting for me and we would carry on to school together, but there was no sign of him. As I walked I kept looking back, expecting to see him running to catch up. But he did not appear. When I got to school I sat in the classroom waiting for him to arrive. Tej did not go to school that day. Or the next.

Eventually, I discovered what had happened. His uncle had hated Tej going into the forest and coming home late when there was so much work to do around the house. He blamed the school and banned Tej from going there for two years. Instead he had to look after his brothers and sisters, and tend to the animals.

Tej lost out on *two* precious years of learning. For a long time I felt guilty about this. It was all my fault. If only I had not said we did not have to go home straight away. If only we had not messed about in the forest. For me school was always very important – and it turned out to be the passport to my future life as an elite soldier.

From a young age I had a winning mentality that meant I wanted to be top of every class. I am proud of what I have achieved – passing all the rigorous recruitment requirements for the Brigade of Gurkhas, and being promoted all the way from Rifleman to the rank of Captain. It is a dream come true. But I did it with hard work. And it all started in that little school in the mountains.

It was not much of a school if you compare it with the schools my children go to now in the UK, with their computers and equipment and organized activities. There were no desks. We sat on the floor. There were no pens or paper to write on. No drawing or painting. There was no proper playground or toys to play with.

For writing I had a small square blackboard that I wrote on with white chalk. To keep the board black I mixed the powder you get inside used batteries with some water and rubbed that on it. We also used our fingers to write in the dust on the classroom floor (we would always be covered in dust, and sometimes mud, at the end of a school day). And if it was a nice day the teacher took us outside and wrote on the ground with a stick.

Near the schoolhouse was a spring of fresh water that I

used to love drinking from in break time. It always energized me. For letting off steam we made footballs or volleyballs from old clothes tied into a ball with rope. We played in the fields in bare feet, and I would sometimes cut my foot or lose a toenail and there would be blood everywhere. We never stopped running. We were always on the lookout for fruit to eat or insects to study.

These are the happy memories I have of schooldays. But I still think of Tej and the time he lost because of his uncle. After two years he was allowed back to school but he had to go back to the grade he had been in before, so now he was two classes below me. He did not seem to have learned his lesson, though. One day, as I was planting corn in our family field, he came up to me and said, 'Hey, Kailash, I've got a good idea – let's go into the forest again!'

'You must be joking!'

'No, it's OK now.' Tej explained that his uncle had got married and moved away to live somewhere else. Now it was down to his mum and dad and they did not mind him going in the forest – especially for the reason he now suggested. 'Let's look for *bantarul*,' he said.

Bantarul is a tuber and root that grows under the ground and is usually found in the steep and inaccessible parts of the forest. You peel and boil it, and it tastes a bit like sweet potato but is even better, in my opinion. It contains lots of protein and was a great favourite of my mother's. She was very religious and on Tuesdays – a day dedicated to Hindu gods – she would fast by not eating salt, chilli or rice. But fruit was allowed – and bantarul if we had any. If I managed to bring some back from the forest I would really be in her good books. It would be a small pay-back for all the things she had done for me.

My mum was not totally pleased about me going into the forest with Tej. The area where we were most likely to find bantarul was quite dangerous with steep cliffs, and rocks that were liable to fall from above. And what she did not know, but I did, was that the land where the bantarul grew actually belonged to someone in the village. If we were caught we could be reported to our parents or even the police.

The idea of having bantarul to eat probably swayed her, but she told us to be careful. I grabbed my little spade for digging up the roots, and strapped my khukuri in a sheath around my waist. And we set off uphill to the edge of the forest. All thoughts of our previous expedition were banished. We were happy.

We made it without incident to the spot where the bantarul grew. It was halfway up a cliff, surrounded by trees. I knew the area well as I grazed my animals here sometimes, and I reckoned we would be fairly hidden as we looked for it. Even so we were nervous as we started our search.

You have to look for the leaves of the plant, which grow up the trunks of trees. It took us a while but then I spotted a tangle of foliage on a giant tree that reached high into the blue sky. There were so many plants there; we had really struck lucky.

We began to dig at the base of the tree, going as fast as we could; sure enough, there were roots all over the place. I had never seen so many. They were big, too – bigger than I had ever seen. I dug them out with the spade while Tej stacked them to one side. Then I came to a big rock that I could see was covering a large bantarul root, one of the biggest I had found.

'Let me just get this last one and that'll be enough,' I said. I hacked at the underside of the rock, trying to roll it out of the way but it would not move. The sun was shining and I started sweating profusely as I gouged the earth under the rock. Then I heard a sound like thunder. The whole cliffside seemed to be trembling. And the rock began to move.

Tej and I jumped to one side just in time. The rock picked up speed and rolled away down the cliff. Followed by another, and another, bombarding the bottom with deafening crashes. We picked up the bantarul roots and held them tight as we watched the rocks smashing down.

Had I started something that would never end? I willed the rocks to stop but they just seemed to get bigger and faster. And if the furious landowner came …

When the rocks eventually stopped falling there was an eerie silence in the forest. Tej and I looked at each other and grinned. We had got away with it! And we had the biggest stash of bantarul you could imagine. It was just a question of how to carry all the roots home. I had an idea – I took off my *sarawul* (traditional Nepalese trousers), knotted the legs at the bottom and filled them with the roots.

Laughing and joking, still pumped up, we started to scramble back down the cliff. I was imagining what my mother would say when I presented her with all this delicious food. As we headed back I saw smoke. Spirals of smoke were rising above the trees. Somewhere in the forest there was a fire. The smoke reminded me of the day I was coming home from school and saw a house suddenly burst into flames.

Those village houses contain a lot of wood and have thatched roofs, so they are easy to set alight. Some children inside had been playing with matches and the whole thing went up. Everyone rushed outside and watched helplessly while their home burned to the ground.

This time the smoke told a happier story. It was coming from a hill overlooking our village, which was a favourite spot for us to play, especially during the festivals of Dashain and Tihar. We used to make a giant swing out of bamboo poles and grass woven into strong ropes, and all the kids would have a great time.

As we got closer we saw that two of our mates had made a fire and were cooking rice pudding in a small pot. They had probably taken the rice without their parents knowing, and some milk from their buffaloes. They offered us some and it was delicious. Food, when it is cooked in the open like this – and you have 'borrowed' it without the grown-ups knowing – is the best ever. There was a gentle breeze to cool us down, and as we ate we were aware of nature all around.

One of my friends had brought up his family's cattle to graze and they were chomping contentedly. Birds were singing, insects were humming. We could hear the roar of the distant waterfall. At times like this I appreciated how lucky I was to live in such a beautiful and simple place.

When we had finished the pot of rice pudding we decided

to prolong the adventure. 'Let's go back in the forest and look for more nice things to eat,' someone said. (OK, it was me!) Tej and I hid the bantarul roots at the base of a big tree, camouflaging them with leaves and mud. We decided it would be OK to leave the cattle where they were for an hour or so. And the four of us went off to the forest.

In the mountains the weather can change very quickly. The sun had been shining, up on the hill. As we walked between the tall forest trees the wind began to shake the branches above us. The sky darkened. There was a clap of thunder, a flash of lightning. More thunder, getting louder, closer. Then the rain.

It drummed through the trees, turned the path to thick mud. The wind blew stronger, so strong that within a few minutes it was splintering the trees. Branches were crashing down around us. Nature, which had appeared so kind and gentle just a few minutes before, had turned into a monster.

Although we were young we had experienced terrible weather before. But this was the heaviest rain and strongest wind we had ever known. We took shelter under a big tree even though we were afraid of it – there's a superstition in our culture that the big trees of the forest like to eat people. That may sound stupid but we did not enjoy standing so close to them.

There was nothing we could do but wait. We looked at each other without saying anything, and listened to the distress calls of the birds and animals through the sound of the wind. We were soon drenched. The tree was not giving us enough shelter so we ran to an even bigger one with a thicker canopy.

The thunder and lightning intensified. The smaller trees around us were breaking in the ferocious wind. The forest floor began to fill with water and it turned into a slow-moving river. This was how mudslides start. If it built up momentum and flowed in the wrong direction, it could wipe away our entire village. Then there were the animals we had left grazing on the hill. If anything happened to them we would all be in big trouble. It seemed a long time ago that we had been happy and carefree up on the hill. Now we felt scared and miserable. I could feel my heart pounding in my chest.

Eventually I made a decision. It might be dangerous but we had to try and get back to the village. 'Come on!' I said to the rest of them. 'We can't just stay here.'

'No way,' Tej said.

We all looked out at the torrential rain, the fallen trees, the mud and flowing water. My friends' eyes were full of fear. 'We don't have a choice,' I said. 'Let's go!' I ran out from under the tree and, thank God, they followed. I tried to steer a path away from the worst of the water and mud. The falling branches missed us. A few minutes later we were back on the hill.

The cooking pot we had used for the rice pudding was knocked over. The fire was covered in mud. Where were the animals? We looked around anxiously. There they were! They had taken shelter by a line of trees. It was probably our imagination but they looked relieved to see us.

Tej and I recovered the bantarul from its hiding place and we all returned to the village as if nothing had happened. Well, nothing much. 'Look at you!' said my mother. She made me promise I would never go out in such bad weather again. But when she saw all the bantarul roots I had brought her she could not be angry.

That evening she cooked me a special meal of pork curry and potatoes and afterwards I went straight to bed. I was completely exhausted by the day's adventures. Before I fell asleep I went through the events of the day. Finding the bantarul. Eating the rice pudding with my friends up on the hill. All just perfect. We should have gone home after that. But no. We wanted more. We were greedy. The forest had taught us a lesson.

CHAPTER 6

NO REST FOR THE WICKED

Deep sleep. My body in recovery mode after the day's fighting at Musa Qala. Then urgent words in my ear. 'Guruji! Guruji!' I sat bolt upright in the camp bed. Looked at my watch. 0300 hours. Ambika stood over me. Time for my sentry duty. I really wanted to burrow back down in the bedclothes and carry on sleeping, like a child. But I was Section Commander. I had to set an example.

'OK. Got it,' I said.

I put on my jacket and grabbed my kit – my weapon, helmet, Osprey (body armour) and HMNVS (Head Mounted Night Vision System), which enabled me to see in the dark.

For the next two hours I patrolled the perimeter of our desert camp with another sentry. Nothing happened. Just a cold wind and those dogs barking faraway.

By 0500 I was back in my bed for a bit more sleep. What seemed like five minutes later it was time to get up. 0600. We followed the usual routine to pack up our overnight halt and 'extracted' at 0635 for the long journey back across the desert to Camp Bastion.

It was an exhausting trip, especially mentally. We had to be on full alert the whole time for possible enemy attacks and IEDs. And it did not help that we were low on drinking water. But we made it back without incident. As soon as we parked the vehicle I jumped out and ran to the accommodation block where I grabbed a big bottle of water and drank it down in one. That made me feel more human. Then I went back to the vehicles to help unload all the kit. I was covered in dust and was feeling completely knackered. But we had successfully completed the resupply mission to Musa Qala. No casualties. Job done.

At that point the Platoon Commander, WO2 Trilochan Gurung, appeared and walked over to where I stood in front of the WMIK. He thought I might like to know where we were being deployed the next day: 'The Sangin Valley.' It was 1700 hrs. We had been in Camp Bastion for fifteen minutes. There is no rest for the wicked!

Sangin DC (District Centre) at that time was the most dangerous district in the whole of Afghanistan. As at Musa Qala, our base there was besieged by the Taliban. They controlled the valley that led to the town and regularly attacked the base with small arms, mortars and RPGs. We were going to be engaged on another re-sup mission. It was a new deployment for us and we were excited to be entering a new part of the country. On the other hand, we knew how dangerous it would be.

We began our preparations straight away. Re-loaded the vehicles, got everything ready to move out the following morning. The Platoon Sergeant, Cpl Shreeman Limbu, gave everything a final check. He briefed us on the details of the mission. By this time it was getting dark and we had to run to the cookhouse as it was about to close. The hot food, a really good curry, tasted fantastic but then again anything would have done as we were starving after the long desert drive. Then it was back to the billets to get rid of all that dust with a hot shower – one of the best showers I have ever had!

I loved that billet because I felt pretty safe there. My bhai-haru were laughing and making jokes. I fell asleep while the light was still on. A deep, worry-free sleep. Maybe I was back in the fields and forests of my childhood with Tej. Then *beep beep beep!* My alarm. *Worse,* I could not understand what was going on. I had never felt anything like this. I felt dizzy, as if my head were falling into a deep ocean. My ears were hurting. I was going to be sick. I could not remember who I was or where I was. I grabbed my head in my hands to stop it spinning.

My mind was blank. I could not think. I tried to move my feet. My right foot would not move. I screamed out: '*Ahhh! Ahhhhhhh!*' Then I realized what was causing the pain. Cramp!

Just cramp. Nothing to worry about. A deep breath. I was Corporal Kailash Limbu, 2 RGR, Camp Bastion, Helmand Province. Afghanistan. About to deploy to Sangin.

I finally tried to turn off the alarm. It was pitch dark in the hut, I could not see a thing and could not locate the clock on the small bedside table. When I finally found it and switched it off I was so tempted to sink back under the bedclothes. The cramp was wearing off. I felt more normal. I just need one more minute in my dreams …

No chance. 'Morning everyone!' yelled Gaj, and switched the lights on. I realized I was still dehydrated from the day before. I drank half a bottle of water and felt ready to face the new day. Whatever it had in store. It was 0445 hours.

Within forty-five minutes we were on the road. It was still very cold, barely above freezing, but the sun was beginning to rise behind the distant hills. My WMIK was leading the convoy. I had Ambika and Gaj with me again. We kept our eyes peeled. None of us said much. It was just another day in the desert.

Hours passed. We saw nothing suspicious. We were all lost in our private thoughts as the endless sand and gravel rolled past. I was thinking of my wife, Sumitra, and my new-born son, Anish. It was not long since I had been in Nepal, holding a tiny Anish in my arms in the moments after his birth. How I missed them all, my daughter, Alisa, as well. How I wanted to hold both my children in my arms and kiss them. Buy them chocolate. Tell them those night-time stories that my mother told me, about the ghosts of the forest.

I really wanted to spend proper time with Sumitra, too. We had been married nearly four years, but had only been together for a total of four months. We were both desperate to go away together, so we could get closer to each other, understand each other better.

I had a similar regret about my parents. We Gurkhas are very family-orientated and my family was particularly close-knit. My mum and dad were so proud of what I had achieved, but I knew that my absence had left a big hole in their lives. This was especially true of my mother.

She just lived to put food on the table in front of me. And I was in heaven when she did – I adored her cooking. I was now a battle-hardened soldier, with seven men under my command. Today my job was to protect the resupply convoy in one of the world's most dangerous conflict zones. Yet I knew that in my mum's eyes I was still a vulnerable child.

Do all the thousands of soldiers currently on active service around the world have similar thoughts as they face life or death situations? All I can say is that always, just before I fall asleep, and as soon as I wake up, and in those crucial moments of battle when I wonder if the next bullet will have my name on it – always, my family is with me in my thoughts and my heart.

I was getting a bit emotional as we drove along. I tried to snap out of it by concentrating on the surroundings. The route I had chosen crossed terrain where there were unlikely to be IEDs and there were few sites of potential ambush. Our biggest worry – the 'legacy' mines left behind after the Soviet–Afghan War of 1979–89.

The empty desert landscapes looked harmless under the morning sun. In fact I was enjoying the peace and beauty of the natural world when a thought struck me. Everybody was following us. The entire patrol was relying on us as the lead vehicle to be going in the right direction. I needed to double-check that was still the case. It was easy to wander off-course in the featureless desert.

So I instructed Ambika to stop the vehicle. Then I checked the map against the magnetic compass. While I was doing this the PRR radio began. It was my Platoon Commander, WO2 Trilochan Gurung, in the convoy behind. Why had we stopped? Did I not know this was dangerous territory? I explained I was checking the accuracy of our bearing. I could now confirm it was spot-on. We continued.

Soon we entered the Sangin Valley, an area of green, irrigated fields. It was beautiful but deadly. The fields were opium poppies. The area was crawling with Taliban and their sympathizers. Our Icom radio scanner was now picking up enemy chatter. They knew we were approaching. The mission was getting serious.

At this point there was a problem in the convoy behind us. We were instructed to stop. The third vehicle from the front, a supply truck, had strayed into a ditch and got stuck. One wheel was spinning in mid-air. The crew of the vehicle worked hard to dig it out. The engine revved, the wheels span. There was dust everywhere. I could smell burning rubber.

It looked like bad news. Everyone waited anxiously. Then suddenly, with a loud clanking, it was free and back on track.

ABOVE At around two years old, sitting between my grandparents outside their house in Khebang village. My parents are standing on the left.

LEFT Aged around seven, on the way home from school with my uncle. School was a thirty-minute walk from home and we always found a reason to explore the forest.

ABOVE A proud moment! I was the champion volleyball player in my village.

LEFT Aged around thirteen, with my little sister Gudiya.

ABOVE My class in Year 10 at school, 1998. I am standing in the middle, in the blue shirt.

BELOW The very next year, in 1999, I was on a field exercise as part of my recruit training with the Brigade of Gurkhas in Aldershot.

OPPOSITE TOP Afghanistan 2002, Balkh Province, during a long-range vehicle patrol. Our unit was known as Provisional Reconstruction Team (PRT).

OPPOSITE BOTTOM Sitting outside the PRT base in the middle of Mazar-i-Sharif City.

TOP At a checkpoint held by Afghani General Dostum's soldiers.

BOTTOM With a local child at a village as we were preparing for an overnight stay.

ABOVE Gaining local information and observing forward ground was part and parcel of our foot patrols.

BELOW Helmand Province, Afghanistan, 2009, returning from Musa Qala after resup. I am standing on the right.

As we moved off my PRR crackled again. Now I was focusing, focusing. Left, right, front. Alert to an attack. It was our Platoon Commander on the radio. According to talk intercepted on the Icom scanner the Taliban were 'getting ready'. But we did not know where, when or how.

Soon, just outside the town of Sangin, our Sangin FOB became visible – just a couple of buildings, a tower and a compound surrounded by a mud wall. This was 2006, early in the deployment of British troops in Helmand Province. But Sangin already had a reputation. By the time the British forces pulled out of Sangin in 2010 to hand over to the Americans more than 100 of our soldiers had been killed there.

Fresh in our memory, as we entered the danger zone on that re-sup mission, was an incident that had happened just a few days before. Special Forces had gone into Sangin on a covert operation to capture four known Taliban leaders. As they returned to their vehicles with the prisoners they were ambushed by a large number of enemy fighters. A platoon of Gurkhas was sent to support them. They too were ambushed.

There was a vicious firefight before Apache helicopters arrived to give them the cover they needed to get back to the FOB. Two British soldiers were killed. One lost his arm after being hit by an RPG. The Gurkhas told me they almost ran out of ammunition, though they still had their khukuris.

As we approached the FOB I felt more and more pumped up. Nervous, frightened, alert. Just like I felt in childhood when I was alone in the middle of the forest and feared that ghosts were coming to kill me. I grabbed my GPMG, mounted on the front of the WMIK. I had been close to death enough times to respect the enemy's strength and cunning. To know they could strike any time.

We entered Sangin. At first the atmosphere seemed normal. The street was full of people going about their daily routine. Shopping, carrying things, just hanging about. I told myself that most of them probably felt friendly towards us. But it was impossible to tell.

None of them waved, which was unusual. In most of the villages we passed through in the desert people were happy to greet us. Now, when some kids chased after us excitedly, their parents tried to stop them. It made sense. The Taliban would probably kill them if they thought they were being too welcoming.

Still, I felt suspicious and vulnerable. I felt eyes watching us from alleyways. I looked everywhere for insurgents. The GPMG was not so good for close-quarter fighting in urban areas like this. I picked up my personal weapon, the shorter-barreled SA80. Rested my index finger on the trigger.

The situation was made all the more tense by the fact that we had to drive slowly to give the rest of the convoy time to catch up. And the alleyways were beginning to seriously worry me. They provided perfect cover for an RPG attack. I noticed now that most of the shops were closed. Something was definitely not right.

On the far side of the street was a field of poppies. It looked beautiful in the sunlight – green and lush after the desert sands. But it was a good place for insurgents to hide. I was expecting to be attacked at any second. But after driving for 300 m, when nothing happened, I began to relax a little bit.

Perhaps it was our lucky day. Perhaps the Taliban fighters were giving themselves a day off. It was possible. By now we were just 75 m from the entrance to the FOB. I could see the walls, the sandbags against them. I even heard the sound of the gate creaking open to let us in. Just a few seconds more and we would be safe inside the compound.

Suddenly, on the right, I saw in the corner of my eye figures running. Women and children. They looked as if they were fleeing for their lives. Then more people running, this time directly ahead of us. What were they all running from? There was an ominous silence.

Then 'Guruji, guruji!' It was Gaj, up on top of the WMIK. He had just spotted a man carrying a weapon dashing inside a building.

'Are you sure?' I tried to keep the panic out of my voice. At critical moments like this it is so important to appear calm, in control. Even if you're not.

'Yes, yes. Over there. In that compound.'

'OK, Gaj. Keep watch.' I raised my weapon, aimed it at the building. I was ready to pull the trigger at the first sign of the enemy. But the most important thing was for the whole convoy to reach the safety of the FOB. If we could get inside we could fight from there much more effectively.

We were now just 20 m from the open gate. I could see our soldiers taking cover inside. 10 m. Getting closer. I thought we were safe.

Then … the crack of a rifle. Just a single round. But a single round is enough to close your eyes forever.

A second later … another round.

Everything seemed to be happening in slow motion. There was no reaction from Gaj and Ambika. No return of fire from our soldiers inside the FOB. I wondered if the Taliban sniper was trying to take us out one by one. I was expecting a third shot when the air filled with a noise so loud it hurt my eardrums. Dust and small fragments were raining on us.

'Bloody hell!' screamed Ambika. He braked hard. The vehicle jolted to a stop. We all put our heads down to protect us from the flying fragments.

'What the hell was that?' I shouted. Ambika and Gaj stayed silent. 'Anybody see anything?' No response. I jumped out of the WMIK. We had stopped next to the compound wall, not far from the gates of the FOB. I looked over it. I saw smoke trails. Dust was everywhere. I could not stop coughing. 'Bloody hell. The bastards!' I knew what had happened. 'RPG!'

There was going to be more where that came from.

'OK, guruji,' replied Ambika. I could hear the fear in his voice. But from Gaj – silence.

The RPG had missed us by a whisker. The PRR crackled. I could not make out who was saying what. I pressed the button and told the Platoon Commander, who was in a vehicle at the back of the convoy, what had happened. More crackles on the PRR. I was not sure if he had understood. There was so much dust I could hardly see the end of my nose.

'Hey, Gaj,' I called. 'You OK?' No reply.

On the battlefield my biggest worry was always the safety of my team. It is the commander's responsibility to get everyone safely back. And for me there was an added incentive – I could not face the prospect of meeting someone's family and having to tell them how their husband or their son, their father or their brother, had been killed alongside me. Ambika, Gaj and I were as close as you can get. I was seriously worried that something bad had happened to Gaj, who was in the most vulnerable position up top on the back of the WMIK.

But before I had time to check on him further we were pinned down under a hail of bullets. There was no let-up. They were striking the mud wall behind us. Clouds of dust bursting everywhere. I knew the gates were just a few metres away but it was too risky to break cover. I had that chilling feeling that I was about to take a bullet. I could not see any possibility of escaping one.

I managed to squeeze back in the vehicle even though it was a soft skin and did not offer any real protection. Then I put my head down – another instinctive reaction that does not actually help but makes you feel safer. There was nothing on the PRR. Nobody seemed to be reacting to the situation. I decided I needed to.

Next to me in the driver's seat Ambika was sitting just like me, head down, hoping to dodge the bullets. 'Ambika,' I said. 'Let's get out of here. Drive to the right.'

No argument. 'Yes, guruji.'

I thought if we moved to the right a bit it would give us a better view of the enemy positions and a greater arc of fire. But we had to be careful. I knew the Helmand River was just a few metres away. If we rolled into that it would be the end for us. I grabbed the GPMG and fired off a few bursts as Ambika prepared to move.

There was another clatter of the machine gun. It took me a second to realize where it was coming from. I screwed my head round. It was Gaj, firing long bursts on the GMG (Grenade Machine Gun) from the top of the WMIK. It was such a relief to know that he was OK. Yet his attack only seemed to intensify the incoming bursts. Our bhaiharu inside the FOB opened up. Then the Platoon Commander came on the PRR. 'Hello 33C. This is 30A. Go firm. I say again, go firm there and provide fire support while the rest of the vehicles get over into the FOB.'

'33C. Roger. Out.'

I yelled at Ambika and Gaj. 'Listen up, bhaiharu. We fight from here till the convoy is inside.' The idea was that we would draw the enemy fire from the re-sup vehicles, keeping the Taliban occupied and our men safe. We quickly located the likely enemy location, a compound about 300 m directly ahead, and targeted it with rapid fire. Me on the GPMG, Ambika with his personal weapon and Gaj on the GMG. Our rounds were landing just seconds apart in the enemy's compound but their gunfire did not let up. Bullets were flying everywhere. I could hear and feel them whizzing past. That fear of being hit, that any second a bullet would find its target, was worse than ever.

While Ambika and Gaj continued to fire I took time to scan the compound with the naked eye. I needed to pinpoint the enemy so we could get a clean and direct hit that would wipe them out. But the dust made it impossible to see with any clarity. Meanwhile I was aware that the convoy had started to enter the FOB. Our plan was working.

Not for long. We Gurkhas do not use bad language except in extreme circumstances. So when Gaj started swearing I knew he had a problem. 'Shit, shit, shit!'

'Gaj, you OK?' No reply. He had stopped firing his weapon. I screwed my head round to get a look at him. I could see him, still holding the GMG, but something was not right. I reckoned he had taken a hit.

'Guruji, is Gaj OK?' yelled Ambika.

'Not sure. Keep firing.'

I tried to stay optimistic. Maybe he just could not hear me in the noise of battle. By now our forces inside the FOB were putting up a huge amount of firepower. On the other hand, maybe he was in so much pain he just could not speak.

Then I caught sight of a man carrying a rifle, running from the corner of the building into the bund-line 150 m away. He took cover and started shooting at us. I aimed the GPMG.

'Enemy, enemy!' It was Gaj shouting. He engaged with his GMG and started firing. Whatever the problem was, he was back on the case. I opened up with my weapon, too. The target stopped firing but enemy gunfire was still pouring down on us from other positions.

I had a mad urge to run forward into the compound where the firing was coming from. To search every inch of the buildings. To hunt down the insurgents and fight them hand-to-hand. But I needed to stay calm. As I checked behind me to see how many vehicles still had to enter the FOB my eye caught suspected enemy movement.

'Ambika, drive forward a bit.' A few seconds later: 'Enemy, enemy, enemy!'

'Where?'

'OK. Listen up. There are two enemy firing on us from one hundred metres. At the corner of the building. Watch my tracer.' I grabbed the GPMG and fired a couple of short bursts. They arrowed in on a spot in the compound wall. Soft explosions and dust. The tracer rounds deflected off hard objects and disappeared way into the distance. 'Bloody hell!' I reckoned I had got them.

'I'm going to kill the Taliban!' shouted Gaj. He engaged the GMG with rapid fire. Ambika was using his rifle. Our world was a little corner of hell yet the two Taliban had not been hit; they were firing back. In fact they had the advantage of the compound walls.

Our fire could not penetrate the compound walls, so we needed to get a direct hit if or when they were exposed while they were in an ideal firing position with a clear view of us. And we made a big static target.

They continued firing. Then they moved again. 'They're running away!' yelled Gaj. They ran into an 3-m-high mud-brick house beside the road. Were they retreating or regrouping? Were they thanking God their lives had been saved, or planning another attack?

The situation reminded me of a few weeks earlier in Now

Zad, another District Centre in Helmand Province where we resupplied the FOB. Insurgents had taken cover in a building. I kept my sights trained on the doorway. If they came out they would come out firing. We had to hit them before they shot at us. We waited. Three minutes. Four. Trying to keep our concentration. It was starting to get dark. We knew they were planning an assault on the FOB. Our translator had picked up chatter on the Icom scanner.

The key was always the network of alleyways. Here the insurgents could move about under cover, launch attacks and just melt away before you had a chance to engage. My eyes were flickering between buildings and across alleyways. I saw a target cross an alleyway and enter a building. I watched and waited. Saw another. I aimed the GPMG. More waiting.

After several minutes a third man appeared, doing what we call 'leopard crawling', low to the ground. We prepared our HMNVS. Kept looking. After a while they opened fire from the building they had entered. And so it went on. Attack and retreat, attack and retreat.

Back in Sangin, the attack was now coming from multiple directions. Our vehicles were continuing to enter the FOB while taking hits from the Taliban fire. But amazingly no soldier had been shot. Even in the heat of battle, when you have a million things to think of, your mind cannot help dwelling on the 'what if?'

What if I were killed? I am an only son. Who would care for my mum, dad and sister? My wife and two young children? It was too much to bear. I had to survive.

My GPMG ammunition ran out. A vulnerable moment. 'Ammo, ammo, ammo!' I shouted. It was an SOP to inform my team so they could cover for me while I reloaded. I asked Gaj to pass over another box of GPMG ammunition. Before I reloaded, I oiled the gun to prevent possible weapon failure.

In intense firefights the barrel sometimes gets so hot it turns red and muzzles can actually snap. So I also changed the barrel. Then I reloaded. This took no more than a couple of minutes. Then I shouted 'Back in!' to indicate the GPMG was ready to carry on firing.

Before I let loose, I had another go at pinpointing the exact enemy locations. With the binoculars I scanned some small buildings about 300 m directly in front of us. There was the glint of a gun barrel. I kept looking. An insurgent appeared at the corner of the building and opened fire. I grabbed the GPMG, aimed, squeezed the trigger. But he was already gone. So frustrating. These people were slippery. They never engaged in direct fighting. They struck and ran away. They planted IEDs. They made booby traps. They were suicide bombers.

I wanted to send them a message. To tell them we were Gurkhas. We were better fighters than them. We trained harder and had braver hearts. We had better weapons and kit. If they would just surrender, we could be friends. We had nothing personal against them. But if they tried to kill us we would kill them first, for sure. Those were the facts.

By now most of the convoy was safe inside the FOB. Then the sound of heavy gunfire. 'What's that, Gaj?'

'Not sure, guruji.'

Ambika continued driving slowly towards the gate of the FOB.

A second later there was an almighty explosion. The top of the building we had been targeting had been hit by mortar fire from the FOB. It disappeared in a cloud of dust and debris. I was pumped up. We were winning. That's what you get if you fight with us! You were asking for it! If you hate us we will hate you back ten times as much!

In the evening light the battlefield was looking like the surface of the moon. Or maybe Mars. The craters. The dust. As darkness fell the rest of the convoy made it inside the FOB; we followed them in and the gates closed.

The feeling of exhaustion was immediate. All that pent-up aggression and fear drained from my body. All I wanted to do was eat and sleep. But first we needed to hand over the supplies. Then we planned for the next day – the route we would take (which had to be different from the one we had come on) and the time of departure.

Finally, we ate – and a quietness descended as we tucked into 24-hour rations supplemented with noodles, chilli and pickle. There were twenty of us in the platoon, another fifteen men manning the base. We had all survived. It went down as a successful day. We could afford to joke about the dangerous moments when we thought we might not make it.

I lay in my cot bed, under a mosquito net. Gulped water. Drank more water. Waited for sleep. I did not exactly feel safe, even in the FOB. We could come under attack from IDF (Indirect Fire) at any time. The slightest noise made me jump.

I thought about the journey back to Camp Bastion the following morning. There might be IEDs and ambushes along the way. A bullet might have my name on it. Somewhere in Musa Qala dogs, as ever, were barking and a donkey brayed. Then I was out like a light.

CHAPTER 7

GHOSTS OF THE FOREST

In April and May 2015, Nepal was hit by earthquakes that killed more than 9,000 people. Fortunately, the district in the northeast where I grew up, and where my family live, was not too badly affected. But it was a catastrophe for the country, and for me it brought back terrifying memories of an event in childhood. When I think back, there was never a time when I did not know danger and disaster.

I was seven years old and could not have been in a safer place so far as I was concerned. I was wedged between the warm bodies of my mum and dad. We were in their bed on the first floor of our cosy mountain house that my parents had built with their own hands, with a little help from my grandfather. No one could have felt happier or safer than me in their bed. I always slept like a baby. Without a care in the world. That night was no different. Then, in the middle of a deep sleep, my father was calling my name, 'Kailash! Kailash!'

At first I thought it was part of a dream. But there was no mistaking the urgency and panic in his voice. He grabbed me by the shoulder. He was shaking me. He was shouting, saying my name over and over again. Part of me just wanted to go back to sleep, to stay where it was safe and warm.

Then I realized I was shaking. Not just because my father was shaking me by the shoulder. I was shaking *anyway*. And the house was shaking. There was the noise of things falling off the shelves. 'We need to go,' my father said.

Mum was making her own noise. She was screaming, '*Sha! Sha! Sha!*' That's how I knew what it was. We believe that when an earthquake comes it wants to take away everything – your house, your wealth, even you. So we ask it go away by saying, '*Sha!*' – an exclamation that we only use for earthquakes.

The house stopped rocking. Then it started again. Items were crashing to the floor. It was pitch black. Dad was fumbling about trying to find the kerosene lamp or a torch. Then we had to find the stepladder that went down to the ground floor.

We were all crawling on the floor, like leopards. Mum told me to hold on to her feet and follow her but I could not find her feet. Then I felt the wicker baskets that we put around the trap door next to the ladder to stop anyone falling through the hole in the dark. I tried to lower myself onto the first rung of the ladder but I missed it.

I fell about 3 m and landed on my back. I cried out in pain. Above me in the dark Mum shouted out, *'Nani, Nani!'*, which roughly means 'Dear son'. I was winded and the pain was so intense I could not speak. I had to remind myself of where I was and what was happening.

Dad came down the ladder and found the kerosene lamp. He lifted me as gently as he could and put me on his back. Then the three of us and our dog Denney rushed out of the house before it collapsed on top of us.

It was just starting to get light. All over the village people were screaming and crying and dogs were barking. Then people fell silent as the sun came up and we could see the damage. Our house had survived. Bits had fallen off it and there was a lot of mess to clear up inside. But my parents were relieved.

Everyone was coughing in the dust. A few houses had collapsed completely and were just piles of rubble and broken walls. The owners walked about in a daze, occasionally picking things up. But we were all really lucky. No one was killed. My sore back turned black and blue but it was nothing serious. And everyone helped to rebuild the houses that were destroyed. Elsewhere in Nepal and India more than a thousand people lost their lives.

I do not think of the earthquake very often. Sometimes when I remember it I think, did that really happen? Did we really go through that? That's how it is with me. I prefer to remember the good times. The bright summer's days, the bamboo trees swaying in the cool breeze, the small birds singing in the banana trees.

Life has never been better than it was then. One day stands out, perhaps because it was after that that the bad things began to happen. I had been sent out to collect firewood, but I got distracted by the sound of the small rushing river near our house. The river was a mystery that fascinated me. So I decided to go and have another look.

The roar of water got louder and louder till I could see the rapids descending the hill in a series of falls. This had to be one of the most beautiful and awe-inspiring places in the whole world, and I had it all to myself. Looking up, I wondered what I always wondered when I came here. How did the water just keep on coming? How long had it been doing this? Was there ever a time when there was no water?

I sat down on a rock above a pool where small fish were swimming in the cool water. A pair of birds landed next to me and started to drink, their tails flicking up and down. Next to the pool were banana trees, bamboo and cardamom bushes that I had helped my family to plant. I could even remember which individual trees I had put in the ground.

Now I grabbed a branch of one of 'my' trees and rubbed the leaves against my face. I think that was the moment when I began to realize how lucky I was to belong to such a place. This native land of mine is still inside me wherever I go. It is even in my name – Khebang, the name of the village, is my middle name.

Reluctantly I left the river that day and continued collecting firewood for the fire. Sometimes I did this on my own and sometimes my mother and my friends would help me. We would gather as much as we could and pile it up for winter. The fire was not just for cooking. It was the only source of heat in the long, cold winters.

As well as collecting fallen dead wood, we sometimes cut down a big tree and chopped it up with an axe and our khukuris. Then it needed to be stacked and dried out properly, over many months. Unseasoned (i.e. wet) wood just does not work. It makes the fire smoke and when it gets in your eyes it is not only uncomfortable but damaging. I've got memories of Mum struggling to cook over the open fire with her eyes streaming from the smoke. She never gave up, though. Food had to be on the table, come what may.

Finding good wood to burn was a constant battle. I went out before and after school but it was never a chore. It was part of village life and it gave me the moments when I felt most connected to my land. One of the places I particularly liked going to was a 7 km trek up the hill from the village.

It was a hard walk but worth it because the views at the top of the hill were spectacular. They always lifted my heart. Down below I could see the roofs of the village, like a model. All around were the snowy peaks of the Himalayas. My favourite mountain, the one that always drew my eye, was Kumbhakarna. To me it looked like a man's head tilted back. I felt that if I stretched out my arm I could touch the man's nose. In fact Kumbhakarna was four or five days' walk away.

But there is darkness as well as light in my memories of

village life. When I was collecting wood on my own I always got scared, remembering the stories of people dying in the forest. There had been quite a few villagers who had died in the forest in mysterious circumstances.

Some people said they had been killed by ghosts. Then they became ghosts themselves and were forced to roam the forest paths looking for people to kill. They did this by pushing them from the top of steep hills or stabbing them with sharp pieces of wood.

My grandfather told me that once, down by the waterfall, he had seen a *ban-manche* (forest man) in the river. These spirits were always on the lookout for children whom they could abduct and initiate in their shamanic ways. The forest man was slightly smaller than a human and most of his body was covered in hair.

When my grandfather saw him he drew his khukuri to fight him. The forest man ran out of the river and that was when my grandfather saw that he had backward-facing feet. This is because the ban-manche is a trickster. If you follow his footprints they will take you in the wrong direction.

When he saw my grandfather's khukuri the forest man shrieked at the top of his voice and disappeared into the forest. My grandfather told me the story as a warning. If I ever came across a forest man when I was alone I would have to fight him or I would be carried off. Apparently a few people had fought the forest men and won. But others who had escaped the clutches of the ban-manche had still died the moment they got home.

So I was always alert when I was collecting firewood on my own. One day I was on my way home with a bundle of wood when I heard my name being called. 'Kailash! Hey, Kailash!' And two figures jumped out of nowhere on the track in front of me. They gave me a shock but then I laughed. It was my friend, Tej, and another boy, Santa, who was a bit younger than us.

'What are you doing?' Tej said.

It was obvious what I was doing. I nodded at the wood.

'OK, we can take that back to your house. Then let's go to the river to play.' He meant the big river, the Tawa, not the small river near my house.

'Yes, let's go to the river,' Santa said. He was jumping up and down with excitement.

I hesitated. I did not have a watch but I could tell from the position of the sun what time it was – about 12.30 pm, time for lunch. Mum would be expecting me back. She and my sister were on their own as my father was then working out of the country, in the Persian Gulf.

'I need to get back,' I said.

'Come on!' said Tej and Santa.

'And I've got to get some grass and food for the cattle.'

I was really torn – for about half a second. If it was a choice between getting hot and sweaty working hard in the forest or having fun by the river, there was no contest. My friends helped me take the wood back to where we stored it next to the house. Then we checked on the cattle. They still had enough to eat. We topped up the water. Then it was just my mother to deal with.

She was cooking as I entered the house. My sister, Gudiya, who was two and a half, was in her little bamboo basket and making those crying noises that meant she was hungry. I had suddenly lost my appetite. I was too excited at the prospect of going to the river with my friends. Tej and Santa were waiting outside while I did the tricky negotiations.

Mum started to serve the lunch, which was rice and daal. I felt nervous. 'Amma, is it OK if I go to the river with Tej and Santa?'

She handed me a full plate of food. 'The river?' she said, frowning. She did not really like me playing near the river. None of the mums did. Some of the places along the river-banks are very steep and dangerous. It is easy to slip and fall. And if you do fall in you do not stand much chance of surviving as the current is very strong.

'*Please,*' I said.

On the other hand she knew that young boys need to learn to look after themselves. She could not keep me in a cage. 'OK,' she said. 'You're a good son. You work hard. You deserve to go and play with your friends. But just watch yourselves, down by that river.'

'Thanks, Mum!'

I hardly ate any food, I was so excited. Before I left I tied a small bamboo basket round my waist. That was for the frogs and fish we were going to catch. I made sure I had my khukuri. Then I went outside and told Tej and Santa the good news. We all did a little dance then headed for our favourite spot on the river, where the fishing was good. On the way we picked up another friend, Dhan. He was a couple of years older than us, a strong swimmer who knew the river like the back of his hand.

Soon we could hear the sound of the water. As we walked through the forest we were chattering away excitedly. Then I noticed that the forest was getting darker. The sky above had clouded over. A strong wind blew through the branches and even the biggest trees started to sway.

There was a flash of lightning and a thunderclap. Very close. I was leading the way with Dhan behind me followed by Santa and Tej. I stopped in my tracks, afraid that if we carried on the lightning would strike us. Tej and Santa looked as terrified as me. Dhan was dead calm. 'Don't worry. It'll be OK.'

Soon the rain began to fall. Big drops that turned into a terrible downpour. Suddenly our little adventure did not seem so exciting. But we carried on, not saying much now. When we reached the riverbank, we saw that the water level was already rising and the current was flowing faster.

We had been planning to fish by hand, feeling the fish out from under the rocks. But the churning water made that more difficult so we switched to Plan B – we used the leaves of a poisonous plant that grows near the river. You crush the leaves up and put them in the water and they temporarily stun the fish, which then rise to the surface. That is the idea and it had worked many times before.

But not this time. Maybe the current was too fast, carrying the leaves away before they could have any effect. We tried again and again. No luck. Meanwhile the rain continued to fall, lightning lit up the sky and thunder bounced off the mountains all around.

'Let's catch some frogs instead,' I said. There is a particular kind of frog that is very tasty and regarded as being highly nutritious. It is generally found in small holes underneath stones on the riverbed. To find the best places we had to wade out into deeper water. Normally we found lots and our baskets would be full. This time we did not catch a single frog.

At this point we would probably have just decided to go home before the weather got any worse. But nature had other ideas, as she often did in the mountains. There was a crash-and-rumble that was louder and longer than a thunderclap. We all look at each other, mouthing the same silent question: what the hell was that? The sky was getting even darker. The thunder and lightning continued to rage. The animals of the forest were crying out in fear.

The awful noise came again – louder, nearer. This time I spoke out loud, 'What was that, my friends?'

They shook their heads and had one last go at looking for frogs. But I knew something was seriously wrong. Then I spotted it; 90 m away, above the riverbank, the earth was moving. The hillside was slowly collapsing with the torrents of water that were pouring down from the upper slopes.

The problem with the river came very quickly. We were standing mid-stream. The water level began to rise. The current flowed faster. It was like a terrible monster that was coming into being. The rushing water made a roaring sound around us, the landslide groaned as if in pain. From the forest came the cries of terrified animals.

I screamed. Then the sound of loud cracks – the land-slide was splintering entire trees and dragging them with it. This brown waterfall was heading for the river in slow motion. Dhan, who was normally the calm one, the one who knew the river best and never got flustered, was hysterical. 'Let's go,' he yelled. 'We gotta go now!'

It was about 5 m from where we stood in the middle of the river to the riverbank. This does not sound much but the water level was rising rapidly. Already it had passed our mid-dles and was rising towards our chests. And the current was getting stronger. Not only that. Just a few metres downstream was the top of a huge waterfall. If anybody went over that they would not survive.

We held hands in a crocodile to steady ourselves and set off for the riverbank – Tej leading the way followed by Santa and Dhan, with me bringing up the rear. The current had already swept us downstream from the shallow part where we had entered the river. We had no idea how deep the channel we now had to cross would be.

We made slow progress. Inching along, our feet feeling their way on the riverbed as we hung on to each other's hands for dear life. But our arms were getting tired. I feared the link would break if the current got any stronger. And if that hap-pened there was nothing to stop us being swept down to the waterfall and death.

We were almost at the bank and I was beginning to think we had all had a lucky escape, when Tej screamed out, 'Santa!'

Tej had let go of Santa's hand. I gripped his other hand as hard as I could to stop him falling under the surface of the water. The water level was now at our chests. Santa was in terrible danger. If I let go now he would not make it. He screamed, 'Kailash *dai*, Kailash *dai*,' begging me to save him, using a term of respect that we reserve for our elders.

Santa was like a younger brother to me. I would have done anything for him. But I was exhausted. I had little strength left in my hand and my grip was weakening. Then another fear. If he did get swept away and I continued to hold onto him, I would be dragged under with him. I did not want to have to make the decision to let him go.

Dhan was steadying me on the other side, but the hand that supported Santa was turning numb in the cold water. I could feel my fingers still weakening by the second. It really was not far to the bank now. Dhan tried to pull me the last few inches and I tried to pull Santa, but we were not making any progress.

I could feel the current pulling my legs, trying to sweep them from under me. The top of the waterfall was now no more than 20 m away and we were being pushed towards it by the strength of the water. It was like one of those dreams when you try to run but it is like running in glue. You do not go anywhere. The river was no longer our friend. It was our sworn enemy and it was trying to kill us.

My body was telling me I could not hold on any longer. The rain was coming down heavier than ever. The pain, the exhaustion, were too much. My mind was screaming at me not to let go. Then I felt our fingers pulling apart. My legs folding beneath me. The current was winning and I had no strength left to fight it. I couldn't save myself, let alone Santa.

As the waters swirled around us my eyes met Santa's. I had never seen such fear and despair in a person's look. And no doubt he saw the same in my face. Dhan and Tej were both screaming at us though the storm was so loud I could not hear what they were saying.

The sky was so dark with clouds it was almost like night. The thunder and lightning raged and the landslide continued its slow rumble. It struck me that even if we reached the river bank we might not be safe for long. If the landslide turned this way it would swallow us up in a second. There have been moments in my life when I believed fate was about to take over and there was nothing more I could do. This was one.

I closed my eyes and thought of Mum and Dad, and my little sister. What would it be like when we slid over the top of the waterfall and plunged down? Would we drown straight-away? Or would we be able to take a deep breath and keep ourselves alive till we hit the bottom?

My body was bent back almost double, like a folded book, as I fought to hang on to Santa and keep my footing in the strong current. Then something changed. Just a tiny bit but it gave me hope. Suddenly there seemed less resistance in Santa's hand. Instead of being pulled away towards the waterfall he was moving towards the riverbank.

When I opened my eyes I saw that Dhan was tugging Santa by the shoulders. Then Tej grabbed him also. We all bundled together and pushed on to the muddy bank. Pulled ourselves from the raging river and just flopped there breathing heavily, unable to speak, for several minutes. The rain soaked us, the mud squelched beneath our bodies. We did not care. We had cheated death. It was a miracle!

But it was not a miracle. When I went over it all afterwards I realized it was Dhan we had to thank. His courage and strength. He never panicked and he somehow found the energy to pull Santa those last few feet to the bank when all seemed lost. It was a valuable lesson for me: never give up, never admit defeat.

The path back to the village was treacherous in the rain. We kept slipping over but eventually we reached a high point on the ridge above the river and were able to look down and see the devastation we had narrowly escaped – the roaring white water, the great brown slick of the mudslide still rumbling on in the rain.

It was dark when I got home. 'Thank God you're back,' Mum said. 'I was getting worried.' Then she looked at me again and said, 'What have you been doing? You're covered in mud. Go and dry yourself off before we eat. Oh, and I've already fed the cattle so you don't have to go outside again.'

I desperately wanted to tell her how close we had come to death. To spill out the whole story of the rain and the mudslide, and being swept towards the waterfall. But I knew that if I did, she would never stop worrying about me – even more than she did already. Every time I went out to collect wood or to play she would worry, especially if the weather turned bad.

And she would probably ban me from ever going to the river again. So I just sat on the floor and said nothing while she prepared the dinner.

Then she noticed the empty basket I had brought back. 'So you didn't catch any fish or frogs?' she said.

'Not today,' I said. 'We were unlucky.'

CHAPTER 8

TAKING THE HILL

My pulse was racing. My heart was pumping underneath my body armour. I was trying desperately to keep my breathing under control. Once again I looked deep into the eyes of my bhaiharu, my seven Gurkha brothers.

'Ready?'

They nodded. We were in no man's land in Garmsir district, Helmand Province. Directly ahead of us at a distance of about 200 m was a hill, about 80 m high, that rose abruptly from the plain. The hill had a compound near its base and was peppered with caves. We had intelligence that the Taliban were hiding out there. Our task was to take the hill and eliminate the insurgents.

It was October 2008. The month before, we had been

deployed to FOB Delhi in Garmsir attached to the 1st Queen's Dragoon Guards. This area was every bit as dangerous as Sangin or Musa Qala. Our base, which was located in the buildings of a former college, came under frequent enemy attack. Now we were on a clear-and-search operation about 16 km south, deep in Taliban territory.

The hill before us was vital ground for our forces. It was from here that the enemy launched their frequent attacks on the base, and its elevation made it the perfect location for Taliban snipers. A previous attempt to capture it had failed. Now it was down to us.

It was 1300 hours on a baking hot day. We were taking cover in the right-angle of a 2.5-m-high compound wall with a number of buildings to our left. I scanned the hill with my rifle sight. It was covered in potential firing positions. I thought about the men who might be hiding in them, men who were intent on killing us and would take pleasure in it. And if we were to kill them, they believed they would become martyrs and be richly rewarded in paradise.

There were stories that when they killed a coalition soldier they liked to cut off his fingers, hands or even legs and extract his teeth. We did not plan on getting killed or captured.

It was nearly time for us to make our move. I looked across at my brothers, wondering what they were thinking. For some it would be their first experience of battle. No doubt they were thinking of their families back home and wondering if they would make it. These were the thoughts that always ran through my head in such moments.

What would happen to my family if I were killed? At the end of each month I sent money back to my parents in Nepal. How would they cope without it? And what about my wife and children in the UK? My children might go off the rails. For my wife the burden would be terrible.

This is what I thought about as I scanned the hill, looking for enemy movement – just a glimpse would be enough to provide a target. Yes, I was nervous. My heart was pumping. But I was also excited and angry. I wanted to get on with it. I wanted to be face-to-face with the Taliban. Then we would see who was stronger, fitter, braver, more committed.

A radio message from the Platoon Commander, Lt Bairsto, '33C this is 30A. You have sixty seconds to move, sixty seconds to move.'

I watched the second hand on my watch ticking down: fifty, forty, thirty … I checked for the final time that the magazine was correctly fitted into the rifle. I placed the safety catch in the 'fire' position, my index finger on the trigger.

Four, three, two, one … We leapt up and moved fast, leaving big footprints in the dust. Weapons pointed at the hill, looking for enemy movement. Ready to fire. My eye was caught by something not on the hill but 200 m to the right of us. A number of people running. They appeared to be males of fighting age. I could not see any weapons. They ran towards the hill and disappeared inside the compound.

Then bullets were fizzing above our heads. It was hard to tell where the enemy were or what their targets were because there were other platoons covering our movement. At least the rounds were missing us by quite a margin.

We were halfway across the open ground between the compound where we had been sheltering and the hill. There were no options to go left or right. We just had to keep running, straight into the bullets. In the corner of my eye I saw more people running. Then I spotted a fighter outside a cave on the hill, dressed in traditional Afghan dress. He fired on us. I fired back, getting off a couple of rounds. Then I dropped.

'Enemy! Enemy on the hill!' I screamed. 'Down, bhaiharu. Down.'

We took up prone firing positions. We were slap bang in the middle of open ground. No man's land. Nowhere to hide. The ground had recently been ploughed, ready to take crops, which made it very difficult to cross. I put down a heavy weight of fire. My brothers joined in. The enemy continued to shoot back. Fire was now coming in from the sides of the hill as well as the front.

The bullets stopped. The enemy were regrouping so we stopped firing to save ammunition. Meanwhile it was getting hotter and hotter. Sweat was sloshing off me. Then the bullets, high over our heads. No problem. 'OK. Fire Team Charlie,' I shouted.

A fire team is a small group of infantry on the battlefield that operates as a cohesive unit. Fire Team Charlie was just me and two colleagues. Team Delta was the remaining four men. We were backed up by 2IC Group made up of Rfn Nagen and three brothers. 'Fire Team Charlie, prepare to move. Move now!' I shouted.

We took a few steps forward while Team Delta suppressed the enemy. Then it was their turn to move while 2IC provided the cover. It was tough going due to the rough terrain. Combat in open ground is basically a killing zone. If you are on it the enemy holds the cards. He has his guns positioned ahead of you, aimed at you. He has cover. To engage him you have to cross that open ground. You can do this as cautiously as you like but you are still putting yourself in mortal danger.

Another fear I had was that the enemy might already be escaping on the far side of the hill. There was no way of knowing because we did not have this area covered by our forces or by ISTAR assets. The Taliban's tactic of just melting away was really frustrating.

By now we had almost reached the base of the hill. I dropped to a kneeling position and scanned the hillside. 'Bloody hell!' I spotted an enemy fighter just as he got off a couple of shots at me. I returned fire but he disappeared. It was impossible to take proper aim in that split second.

My seven bhaiharu were now alongside me, lying in firing positions, covering the top of the hill. More gunfire rattled over us. I felt very exposed. I had never taken a bullet but I had seen plenty of others who had. I knew it would be painful. But the bullet that puts you to sleep forever – maybe that one you do not feel? That's what I was wondering.

There was another danger: IEDs. It was likely the Taliban had deployed IEDs to protect the hill. A single device could easily wipe us all out – or at least cause heavy casualties. I had several colleagues who had lost limbs to IEDs. From the enemy point of view the improvised roadside bomb was a hugely successful weapon that not only caused a lot of casualties but struck fear in our hearts.

The problem was that they were almost impossible to detect with the naked eye. On this occasion the terrain was already churned up and the enemy were good at disguising where they buried them. That's why we used metal detectors, though they were not foolproof. Sometimes the Taliban used minimal metal in their construction and the detectors did not pick them up.

Before we progressed into the heart of enemy territory, I had to decide whether to check for IEDs. Time was not on our side. If we were to stand any chance of capturing the enemy on the hill before they got away we needed to move fast and aggressively. By checking for hidden devices we would lose precious minutes. Plus, we would make ourselves easy targets while we operated the metal detectors. On the other hand, if we just ploughed on regardless – if we took that gamble – it not might not end well. Such are the split-second, life-or-death decisions you have to make in the heat of battle. I decided to plough on.

In my pocket I kept the lucky coin my mum had given me. To bring me luck. To deflect enemy bullets. Now I touched it. Then, taking two men with me, I started to climb the hill. Rifle to the fore. The rest of the bhaiharu stayed back, under the command of 2IC.

These were tense moments. It was a real challenge to climb the hill while looking for the enemy and keeping the rifle ready to fire. In all that heat, with fear and tension running through me, I felt exhausted. Not as sharp as I needed to be. And it was not just me I was responsible for. I was leading my brothers into the jaws of the enemy. If I made one false move or failed to act fast enough they would suffer the consequences of my mistake.

A flash of movement. Two fighting-age males running down the hill to the compound at the bottom. Then gunfire. Just as the bullets flew around us I lost my footing, fell over and began to slip back down the hill.

'Guruji, you OK?'

I tried to grab hold of something on the ground to stop my fall but there was nothing. I kept sliding, for about 10 m. I was nearly back to where we had started at the bottom of the hill. There was a searing pain in my back and blood was coming from my knee.

The two bhaiharu with me started to crawl back down the hill to help, but I waved at them to stay where they were. Behind us, 2IC put up covering fire as I climbed back up the hill. It was painful but I rejoined my brothers and we carried on climbing.

An explosion and a scream. 'Everything OK?' I shouted to the two men behind me. No reply. I kept focused on the slope in front. 'All good back there?'

'OK, guruji. We're right behind you.' At that moment one of them slipped. The other hauled him back up. We kept going. We were almost at the top. Now I was totally focused wondering what we would find there. I had my khukuri at the ready to use at close quarters if necessary. Far better than a bayonet. Easier to handle and it was in my blood.

I hit the top of the hill running. The ground flattened out and breathtaking views opened up, of a village below and a green zone to the south. Then a burst of bullets over my head. Down in the compound a man was running from one side to the other. My view was partially obscured by the compound buildings, but I reckoned he was the one who had just tried to kill me.

My two bhaiharu joined me and carefully, trying not to present too much of a target to the enemy, we started to clear the enemy positions and caves we found up there. There were recent footprints and empty ammunition cases that showed this had been an enemy stronghold. All the time I had my finger on the trigger, expecting one of them to pop up any second. And if he did, I would put him down.

More incoming fire. More accurate this time. 'Take cover!' I shouted. We jumped into a fire trench dug by the enemy. The bullets were too close for comfort, coming from a cluster of buildings about 150 m away from the hill. We did not return fire because we could not tell where the enemy were firing from. If we just blasted away we risked killing innocent people, and it would be a waste of ammunition.

A few minutes later, the 2IC's group arrived on the top of the hill and we continued to clear the area. In a large cave we found bedding and blankets that suggested the enemy used it to rest and sleep in. So near yet so far. It was frustrating.

My assessment was that they did not want to fight us face to face. When they saw us coming they had retreated from their well-defended hill to that cluster of buildings. This was typical. They rarely stayed to fight us in the open, relying instead on guerrilla tactics of hit and run, and those terrible IEDs.

But we had at least accomplished what we set out to do. We had captured the hill, we had achieved our LOE (Limit of Exploitation). These trenches up on the top were where their snipers had caused so much grief to our forces. Now we occupied them.

For twenty minutes we held firm on the hill to ensure there was no imminent enemy threat from an unexpected quarter. In that time we took no incoming fire. With my binoculars I scanned the surrounding area on all sides for enemy movement. I concentrated on the village. There were plenty of people down there but they were going about their daily business. No one fired on us. I began to relax, and that was when the exhaustion hit me.

A few minutes later we received orders from the Platoon Commander to extract to base. The sun was beating down. I was dripping with sweat. The water in my CamelBak hydration pack had almost run out. We were allowed a five-minute water break before leaving the hill. I was just cooling off, taking sips of water, when we received another instruction to withdraw.

We used the same route back, running fast. News came through on the PRR that an IED had been found in the area. A few minutes later we heard the controlled explosion as the IED team blew it up. We reached the vehicles and they took us back to FOB Delhi. It was almost dark by the time we got there. After dinner we cleaned our weapons and cleaned our bodies, ready for the next day. Then we discussed about the IED; it turned out it had been located exactly where me and my seven brothers had taken up firing positions at one point. One of us had probably lain down on top of it.

CHAPTER 9

RIVER OF DEATH

For two weeks after our close shave at the river I did not dare to go back there with my friends. It took me a few days to properly recover from the ordeal. My hands were shaking. My body felt peculiar. I was permanently nauseous and my morale was low. I could not believe Mum did not notice that something was wrong with me. I just concentrated on getting back into the daily routine.

Before school, I looked after the cattle. In school, I worked hard at my studies. In the evenings I fed the cattle again and stayed with Mum to help her in the fields next to the house, where we grew potatoes, maize, wheat and cardamom.

I started to feel like the old Kailash. And eventually I did return to the river with my friends. We even caught fish and frogs but we were very wary. We never forgot that we had almost died that day. We never forgot how dangerous the river could be. We were always looking over our shoulders to check that the weather was not about to ambush us again.

Food was a big deal for me then and still is now – my wife's home cooking makes me so happy and it is what I miss more than anything when I am away! I loved us all eating together as a family. But I also loved sneaking off with my friends to eat things without our parents knowing. I have mentioned making the rice pudding on the hill. We also took eggs and potatoes from our homes and had picnics in hidden places where we would never be found.

Food never tasted better than this – except maybe in Afghanistan after a day of hard combat when I returned to base; so hungry and thirsty I could have eaten a horse and drunk a month's supply of water in one go.

Other wonderful memories of childhood include when Tej and Santa would sleep over at my house. Then we stayed up most of the night, whispering about the things we liked best. Forest food like walnuts and castanopsis nuts. Catching fish and frogs. Bullfights! These were when we took our bulls into the forest and made them fight each other. They never did much harm to each other but our parents would have been angry if they had found out.

So the year passed. My sixteenth year on this earth. And we came to that month when the weather is perfect and everything is in balance. October: warm but not too hot in the day, cool but not cold in the evenings; the rice nearly ready to harvest. Rice paddies are one of the most beautiful sights of Nepal, with nicely curved terraces of bright green rice climbing up valleys and hillsides, glowing in the sun.

At this time we clean and paint our houses so they look spick and span. We clear the paths through the village and between the houses. We put on new clothes. For this is the time most of us look forward to more than anything in the entire year: the Hindu festival of Tihar.

This festival of light goes on for five days, celebrating the connection between people and nature. Nepali and Hindu people celebrate it right across the world, wherever they may live. But up in the mountains it is an unforgettable experience. We put candles and small lights inside and outside our houses so the whole village is illuminated like a magical kingdom. And the children form dancing and singing groups and parade around the village.

Tej, Santa and I loved all this singing and dancing. Often we were joined by a beautiful girl called Benuka, the sister of Dhan, the brilliant guy who had saved our lives down on the river. She was slightly older than us, about seventeen. Sometimes we called her *didi*, meaning 'older sister' and sometimes *phupu*, meaning 'auntie'. I knew her well as we often worked side-by-side in the fields planting and harvesting rice.

One day, during the Tihar, I was sunbathing on a big flat stone just outside our house and gazing up at the blue morning sky. A solitary white cloud was floating across and I was following it, thinking how nice it would be up there.

I closed my eyes and drifted off to sleep. The festival was brilliant but exhausting, and I had got up early that morning to plant corn in the field before we started the day's celebrations. Then, in my dream, I heard a voice calling. 'Kailash *dai*! Kailash *dai*!'

The voice stopped and I carried on sleeping. Then it came again. Louder, more urgent. I opened my eyes. Santa was standing in front of me. I could see he was pumped up, anxious. 'What's up?' I said.

He did not speak at first but his hand was waving up and down. He just could not get the words out. Then he spoke. 'It's Benuka didi…' he said. Benuka had gone missing. Her father had noticed very early in the morning that she was not in their house. He had gone out to search for her. Other villagers had joined in. They were concentrating on the river because she was last seen heading in that direction – towards the dangerous stretch that we had had the lucky escape from a few months before.

I rushed inside to tell my mum, who was as shocked and worried as I was. Then I set off for the river with Santa and a crowd of other villagers to help with the search for Benuka. As we got near the river we could hear the sounds of the falls.

Insects buzzed, leeches were attacking our legs and the air became humid. The vegetation got so thick it was hard to walk through. Stinging nettles stung our legs. I wanted to cry out but managed to keep quiet. There were more important things to think about. I wanted to believe we would find Benuka and she would be OK. But I had a bad feeling.

There was a long crocodile of us walking through the forest. Through the trees ahead the daylight was getting brighter and the sound of the waterfall was now so loud we could not hear ourselves talk. We came out on the top of a cliff overlooking the falls.

In front of me and all around grown-ups from the village were standing, blocking my way. Some were talking – shouting into each other's ears – but I could not hear what they were saying. Others just stood and stared. I squeezed my way to the front.

When I saw what had happened, I stopped dead in my tracks. Santa was pushing me from behind. He could not see what I could see. My hands started shaking. Then my whole body.

'What is it?' said Santa.

I had no words. Below us, on the steep bank about 45 m above the river, Benuka was hanging by the neck from a bamboo rope tied to the branch of a tree. Her body was twisting slowly in the breeze. Her flip flops had fallen off her feet and were lying below her on a rock. Next to the flip flops was her bamboo basket. As usual she was wearing a lovely dress – a traditional golden-coloured *kurta suruwal* with a red scarf. The awful thing was, if you looked at her from a certain direction she could just have been standing there admiring the waterfall.

Her mum and dad and other close family members were standing near me. They were crying and beating their chests. They were so weak from the anguish that they could hardly stand, and friends were holding them in case they stumbled and fell over the edge of the cliff.

My friend Dhan was with his and Benuka's mum. I went up and hugged him. No words. We just wept. Looking at her dangling body and trying not to look.

The police arrived from their office near the school. They cut the body down. Then the family took over and carried the body to the graveyard further up the cliffs with everyone following. Some villagers made a pyre of firewood and the body was placed on top. Then, slowly, people covered it with branches and lit it.

The fire took a while to catch. I was standing with Santa, next to Dhan and his parents. We watched the flames, saying nothing. Soon they were shooting up in the air. I thought of the times I worked in the fields next to Benuka. We would chat and joke. Sometimes she gave me some of her food, or tea. Now she was disappearing in the flames. The world really was hard to understand.

The fire slowly burned down, but it had not quite done its job of destroying the body. It was stoked up again till it burned brightly once more. We continued to watch, thinking of Benuka, paying homage in our hearts to her and her family. Soon she was just dust. And it was starting to get dark. It had been a long and terrible day.

Dhan escorted his parents and family friends back to the village. Santa went off with his father. I was left alone. It was about 2 miles back to my house. I set off through the forest. Visibility was poor and I stumbled along. In the distance dogs were barking. Crickets were humming in the trees, frogs were croaking in the undergrowth. I started to feel peculiar. My shoulders and head felt as if they were growing bigger and bigger.

Then I had to stop as I could no longer see the path ahead. It was nearly pitch dark. I heard voices behind me and assumed some people were approaching so I waited for them. Maybe they had a torch, although I could not see any light. The voices stopped.

Then I heard a rushing, moving sound as if someone was running fast through the undergrowth. Running to escape from something – that is what I thought. I was scared to death by this stage. I shouted out: 'Who is that? Is someone there?' There was no reply.

I knew I could not just stay there, rooted to the spot, scared out of my wits. I started to move forward, holding my hands in front of me in case I bumped into anything. The voices started up again. The feeling of being followed. I was thinking they were ghosts. The forest ghosts we all heard so many stories about and were so scared of.

Slowly, slowly, I made progress. The visibility improved a bit as I neared the edge of the forest. Then I came to a house that belonged to a nice lady who I used to call grandmother, though she was not part of my family. It was late by this time, about 10 pm, but I knew she would not mind if I knocked on her door.

Sure enough, she invited me in. I told her what had happened, and she said I should stay the night and go the rest of the way home in the morning. But my mum and sister were on their own as Dad was still working abroad. I said I needed to get back as Mum would be worried. I sharpened a dried bamboo stick with my khukuri, lit it in the lady's fire so it gave off a bright glow and carried on.

I felt more scared than ever. Now it was not just the ghosts that bothered me. I kept imagining Benuka, hanging from that branch. She was straight in front of me on the path. She was talking to me, offering me tea or water. She was also behind me, following.

I came to an area where tall bamboos grew. They were swaying in the breeze, making a loud swishing noise that terrified me. Rationally I knew what it was. But I could not help thinking that the forest ghosts were trying to communicate with me through this noise. They were trying to get inside my head. Benuka would not leave me alone either. I could feel her presence. She had become one of the ghosts.

My house was now fairly close. I gripped the bamboo torch even tighter and ran as fast as I could. The flame was beginning to die out. Would I make it back home before it went out and left me in darkness again? I remembered what my grandfather had told me about the forest ghosts, that they could kill fire. Perhaps that was what was happening. The ghosts were playing one last trick to capture me, before I reached the safety of home.

The flame finally went out when I was still about 300 m from the house. But I had reached our field, and knew the way, even in the dark. And then my beloved dog Denney appeared, barking his head off, so happy to see me – though not as happy as I was to see him.

My mum and Gudiya had been waiting up anxiously, and Mum hugged me close as we talked about the terrible thing that had happened to Benuka. The terrible thing that she had done to herself. There was food left out for me and she urged me to eat, but I was not hungry and barely touched it.

I went to bed but could not sleep. The events of the day churned around in my head. The image of Benuka hanging from the tree, her body slowly turning, kept flashing in front of my eyes. I prayed to God that she would find the peace in the other world that she had not found in this one. I thought of all the things she had wanted to achieve – getting married, having children – that would be left undone. Maybe she would achieve them in heaven. I hoped so with all my heart.

Then I started asking myself the obvious question. Why? What terrible things had happened to her to make her want to take her own life? Benuka was very honourable and highly respected. Everyone had liked and admired her. Afterwards there was a rumour about her and a boy in the village.

Apparently they had been discovered together, which would have been shaming for her. And he had belonged to a different caste, which made things worse. People said she was full of remorse, not wanting to bring disgrace on her family, so did what she thought was the honourable thing. If that was the case it would have been typical of Benuka didi. She always put others before herself and the world is a poorer place now she is gone.

That night, when I eventually fell asleep, thoughts and images of Benuka haunted my dreams. When I woke in the morning I felt sad and frightened and it took many days and weeks for me to get over Benuka's suicide, and for life to settle back down into something like normal.

One evening, about two months after that tragic day by the river, I was feeding the cattle when I saw Santa running along the top of the hill near our house. I thought he was just messing about with friends, but a few minutes later he turned up at our house out of breath and very upset. 'Hey Kailash,' he said. 'Guess what? Now Dhan has gone missing. Same place. Down by the river.'

It was hard to believe. Our dear friend, our guide and teacher of how to catch fish and stay safe on the river, had not been seen since the day before. His family and some other villagers were already out looking for him. They were searching along the river, the very place he knew so well and loved so much.

It was impossible to think that anything bad had happened to him. Not to Dhan of all people. Not on the river. 'Maybe he's gone to stay at a friend's house,' I said. This was in the days before mobile telephones. He would have had no way of contacting his parents to tell them he had decided not to come home that night.

Still, we needed to go and help with the search and find out what had happened to our dear friend. I told Mum what we were doing. She tried to make me eat something before I left but I was not hungry. I was too knotted up. I grabbed my torch and Santa and I set off. It was about 6 pm and darkness was falling.

On the way we met a senior and respected villager who had decided to join the search, and the three of us made our way through the forest. The darkness was now complete, but my small torch produced just enough light to illuminate the path. None of us spoke much. We were wondering about Dhan. We were also worried about ghosts. Every so often I would turn and flash the torch behind me in case we were being followed.

We reached the river and crossed it on a wooden bridge. On the top of the hill on the far side we could see lights and hear people's voices. Someone called out, 'Who's that?'

'Kailash!' I called back.

'OK. Come up here.'

I was hoping to find Dhan at the top of the hill. He would be telling everyone where he had been and having a joke. There was a group of about ten villagers including Dhan's father and brothers. But no Dhan. 'So where is he?' I asked one of his brothers.

He did not reply but his eyes filled with tears. Then he pointed outward into the darkness. I stepped forward and shone the torch where he was pointing, at the cliff to one side of the hill. I could not believe what I was seeing. I took a step back and flopped down on the steep ground. I just sat there, my whole body trembling.

I shone the torch again to be sure. Dhan's body was lying between two trees at the edge of the cliff, his head facing down towards the river and waterfall many metres below. His khukuri was hanging from his belt. It looked as though he had fallen from higher up and the trees had broken his fall.

The other villagers reckoned he had been tending to some cardamom bushes up on the hill and decided to have a cigarette break. One of his favourite spots was a place where there were several large flat stones. The most likely explanation was that the stone he was sitting on came loose, and he fell head first down the hill as far as those trees. He must have hit his head along the way. Then the loose stone fell on top of him. 'He would have died instantly,' someone said.

We all stayed there the whole night, guarding the body from wild animals. I slept a bit. But awake or sleeping Dhan was in my thoughts. All the adventures we had had together. How he saved my life in the river. Sometimes I was laughing to myself and sometimes crying.

In the morning Dhan's father and brothers recovered the body with the help of villagers and laid it out on the hill. Then two dhami arrived. When someone has had a 'bad death', such as a violent accident, we believe that their souls need to be separated from the evil spirits that caused their death. Only the dhami can perform the rituals to cleanse a dead person's soul.

The dhami shook their bodies, chanted and hit copper plates over Dhan's corpse. At one point one of them actually leant down and bit Dhan's body a number of times. This is how they extract all the bad spirits. Then we carried the body down to the river and built a funeral pyre on the river bank to cremate the body. As the smoke drifted up into the trees a little bit of me died with Dhan.

After his death – so soon after Benuka's suicide – life was never the same again. Tej, Santa and I did not go to that stretch of the river again. We never again set foot on the path through the forest that went down to the river. We were suspicious and fearful. We had lost our innocence. We knew how cruel life could be.

There was a postscript to this story that happened several years later, in 2002. By that time I was in the Brigade of Gurkhas and based in Folkestone. I was returning to Nepal on leave and it was to be a very special visit – I was going to meet my future wife, Sumitra, for the first time.

The marriage had been arranged through my grandparents. There was already a family connection because her uncle, also a Gurkha, was married to one of my aunts. Sumitra and I were not complete strangers. We had exchanged letters (no email then – our letters could take months to arrive) and spoken on the phone a few times. We got on very well from the beginning. But meeting face-to-face was something else. I had brought lots of presents for everyone, including clothes, handbags and jewellery for the women.

It was a tiring journey, by plane from London to Delhi, then a connecting flight to Kathmandu and finally a short domestic flight to where my uncle lived, near Jhapa Charali. My grandparents were waiting for me at my uncle's house. So were Sumitra and her parents. I was nervous of course and I probably did not look my best after such a long journey. Sumitra seemed shy but looked lovely, dressed in a pink kurta suruwal. Our families fussed around us and soon we were smiling and everyone relaxed.

From the first moment, Sumitra and I clicked. I handed out the presents, which went down well. Sumitra's parents gave their blessing to the marriage. We ate some food. I could have slept for a week by this point but it was soon time to get on the road again. The following morning my grandfather, Sumitra and I hired a 4×4 and I drove to my home village of Khebang where my mum and dad, and a big group of family and friends, were waiting to greet the newly betrothed couple.

The journey was long and tiring but we were all in good spirits and looking forward to the celebrations that would take place when we got there. It would be the first time in three years that I had been back to the village. Apart from the marriage celebrations I could not wait to meet up with my old friends again. I had brought them all presents from England. I hoped they would like them.

When we got there the house was filled with light and laughter. It was a wonderful homecoming. I was so happy to see my mum and dad and sister again. I was proud to show off Sumitra to them and to my friends. And I was proud to show her my family home. After all the introductions we ate some wonderful food – potato curry and daal – cooked by Mum. Finally, towards the end of a long and exhausting day, I managed to get Mum on her own for a quiet chat.

I told her how well she looked and asked her about my father. She said they were both in good health and spirits. We talked about Sumitra, my future wife, and arrangements for the wedding. Then I asked her about my friends and she went very quiet. 'Mum, what is it?' I said.

'I have some bad news, Kailash. Santa is dead.'

'*Santa?*' I couldn't believe it. 'How?'

'He drowned.' She said Santa had been fishing and must

have got swept away by a strong current. Villagers found his body washed up on the river bank.

I could not believe it. I was in shock. Surely it was not the same river where Dhan and Benuka had died? Where the four of us – Dhan, Tej, Santa and I – had almost drowned? After Dhan's death we had sworn we would never go near it. No. My mum said it was somewhere else, a river much further away that took four or five hours to walk to. That was the tragedy of it. He had avoided the 'bad river'. He thought he was being sensible.

'But I brought him a present from the UK,' I said. It was a smart shirt. I had been really looking forward to giving it to him and seeing his face light up.

CHAPTER 10

LOSING A
BROTHER

There is no closer bond between Gurkhas than that between soldiers who joined up together. There is even a word for it: *numberi*. My closest numberi was called Yubraj Rai. The last time I saw him was in the downdraught of a Chinook helicopter at the HLS (Helicopter Landing Site) at Camp Bastion in the summer of 2008. He was about to deploy to Musa Qala in the north. I was going south to FOB Delhi, near Garmsir. Before we went our separate ways we shook hands.

Our connection went back to Pokhara, in the centre of Nepal, where we were side by side for the gruelling final selection process for joining the Brigade of Gurkhas. After more than three weeks of doing medical, physical and educational tests together we were like brothers. Luckily we were both successful. And when we flew to the UK to start our army careers we sat next to one another on the plane.

Those journeys by plane stick in my mind as it was the first time I had flown. Flying over the Himalayas we were seeing the mountains from above for the first time. Previously we had only looked up at them. Then there were the rice paddies making beautiful patterns on the green hills, sometimes all the way to the very top. I found it hard to believe I was in a structure that was far bigger than my family house, yet it was flying through the air.

I was so naive that the toilet on the plane confused and frightened me. It was so small. And I certainly was not going to lock the door in case I got stuck in there for ever. Of course I did not dare say anything to anybody – even to Yubraj. Much later he told me that he had thought the same thing – he had not locked the door either!

On the flight to the UK I started feeling very homesick and my eyes filled with tears. I was not yet eighteen years old. This was only the second time I had been away from my mum, dad and sister. The first time I had been in a plane and the first time I had been outside Nepal. I knew Mum would be heart-broken, too. On the other hand she was so proud of what I had achieved. And my leaving meant a much better future for the whole family. There were mixed emotions for all of us.

It was a great comfort to have Yubraj sitting next to me as these feelings swept over me. And when we got to England we stayed together for nine months while we did our training at Queen Elizabeth Barracks, Church Crookham, near Fleet in Hampshire. We ate together, listened to music together, helped each other out in tight situations. And by the end of that period we had forged a bond of friendship that would never be broken. Since then we had been posted to different places, but we always kept in touch and occasionally met up. When I ran into him at the HLS at Camp Bastion we could have chatted for hours, but the military timetable had other ideas.

'C'mon, guys,' yelled the loadmaster of the Chinook. 'Let's go. It's getting late.' The rotor blades were battering us with wind and dust. We could hardly hear ourselves speak. We shook hands one more time. Yubraj gestured to the rest of his team. They picked up their fighting gear and walked over to the helicopter. Before he boarded he smiled, lifted his hand and waved back one final time. I can still see him, hand raised, at the back of that Chinook.

He went north and I went south. By this time I was a section commander, in charge of eight men. Over the next few weeks we were fully occupied in fighting insurgents on ground patrols, clear-and-search missions and resupply missions. One afternoon we had just returned to FOB Delhi after a routine patrol when one of my bhaiharu, Rfn Raju, came up and offered me a bottle of water. It was straight from the fridge, just what I wanted. 'Thanks,' I said.

We stood there for a minute drinking water, not saying anything. Then Raju spoke. 'I have some bad news, guruji ...' He told me that my dearest numberi, Yubraj Rai, had been killed by the Taliban. He had received a fatal gunshot wound on an operation south of Musa Qala.

This was difficult information to accept or process. I stopped drinking the water. I held my head in my hands and closed my eyes. I was having to force myself to breathe deeply and slowly to stop myself collapsing. The memories came flooding in as if playing on a screen in my mind. Over and over again I saw him standing at the back of the Chinook that final time. Waving. Smiling. And suddenly I was crying.

It was not just the memories. Yubraj had had plans for the future. After the tour he intended to find his soul mate to marry and settle down with. Then he would be able to invite my family over to his house, as he had been many times to mine. Maybe one day our two families would go on holiday together (we had talked about Disneyland Paris). And he dreamed of being a father – how we would be able to watch our kids playing together as we drank coffee and chatted about old times.

All these plans and dreams were destroyed in a split second. I felt angry. I felt broken inside. But I dried my eyes. I tried not to show how badly it had affected me in front of my junior bhai. That evening I hardly ate – just a few pieces of fruit. I lay awake most of the night. The following day I returned to Camp Bastion by helicopter to say my final farewells to Yubraj.

It was early evening in the TLZ (Tactical Landing Zone), an area next to the camp designated for the take-off and landing of transport aircraft and helicopters. A searchlight illuminated the scene. A C130 Hercules was on the tarmac, props turning, ready to return to the UK with the body of Rfn Yubraj Rai of the 2nd Battalion The Royal Gurkha Rifles. A guard of honour stood in two lines, waiting to salute his departure. I stood to one side with the rest of the soldiers.

The moment arrived and I was not sure I could cope with it. An ambulance slowly approached the back of the Hercules with hazard lights flashing. The bhaiharu who had been selected to carry the coffin opened the doors of the ambulance. My numberi's coffin was draped in the Union Jack. They hoisted it onto their shoulders and carried it slowly towards the aircraft between the two lines of men.

I watched the coffin approach. I wanted more than anything to see Yubraj's face for one last time, to give him one final hug. As it came alongside me I could not control myself any longer. I started to cry. It was as if his soul could see into mine and knew how I felt. All our plans turned to blood and dust.

The coffin was placed in the Hercules. I took one last look at Yubraj before the doors closed and the big plane swallowed it up. The C130 taxied, turned and rumbled into the air in a cloud of dust and noise. I watched it getting smaller in the evening sky. I raised my hand and said in my head, 'Take care my friend. Safe journey.'

Early the next morning I returned to FOB Delhi where I carried out routine daytime patrols, and tried to distract myself from thinking too much about Yubraj. After a few days I had to return to Camp Bastion to pick up supplies for the base. I was in the little coffee shop there, buying a cup of coffee, when I ran into a Gurkha brother, Lance Corporal Gajendra Rai, who had been Yubraj's 2IC.

'How's Gajendra bhai doing?' I asked him.

He shrugged. 'I'm OK. It's been very quiet. We're just getting on with things. Since Yubraj was killed …' His voice trailed off.

We looked at each other. Gajendra got a coffee and we sat down to talk. 'So what happened?' I asked.

'It was a clear-and-search operation. The whole battle group was involved. Roughly 1030 to 1100 hours. We were knackered. Had hardly had any sleep. Pushing the enemy back non-stop. House to house, door to door.' He paused. 'Our Section Commander yells, "Prepare to move. Move now, move now!"'

Gajendra used his hands to show me what had been happening on the ground. They were ordered to push on and reach the cover of a compound from where they could launch more attacks on the enemy. To get there they had to cross a field with no cover. 'As we were running, I heard something like the sound of a mini-flare,' he said. 'I was thinking it was friendly C/S [i.e. friendly fire]. A couple of seconds later one of the rounds picked up dirt right next to us. Then I knew it was an enemy sniper engaging.

'We ignored it. Kept running. But the bullets were flying. It was one of the worst ambushes I've been in. Hard to believe no one was going to get hit. But hey, this is what we train for.' Gajendra said the men dropped to a prone position and returned fire. They had no cover. They could not identify the enemy's movements. They were sitting ducks. 'It was like being in a snow storm,' was how he put it.

'Staying there wasn't an option. The section commander issued another order to move. So we stand up in the middle of hell. Bullets are flying all around. Striking the ground next to our feet. There's another seventy-five metres to reach the compound. I'm thinking it's fifty-fifty whether we make it or get hit. So we get there. Take cover behind the compound wall. Start returning enemy fire.'

Then Gajendra noticed that two men were missing. Yubraj and Dhan had been left behind on the open ground. He looked back. 'They were trapped. Right in the middle of the fire zone. Their heads were down but they were still trying to get off some rounds. We were trying to fight back but it was hard to see the enemy. It was chaos. Gunfire blazing in all directions.'

Gajendra shook his head, reliving the scene. 'They decided to make a dash for it. They stood up. And in that split second Yubraj fell down again. He screamed. We knew straightaway he had been hit. Dhan shouts, "Casualty! Casualty!" Bullets are hitting the ground all around them. Yubraj is not moving. Dhan goes back down and returns fire.

'The situation was desperate', Gajendra said. It had been impossible to have any control over events. The enemy had a clear view of them. They had no clear picture of where the enemy were firing from. It did not help that the Platoon Commander alongside Gajendra, 2nd Lt Cochrane, had had his radio knocked out by an enemy round. In fact it was a miracle the bullet had not killed him.

Gajendra handed his radio over to Lt Cochrane so the PC could issue orders and co-ordinate a response. Gajendra had his own plan to execute. He grabbed his colleague, Rfn Manju Gurung, and looked him in the eye. 'We're going to extract

Yubraj,' he said. 'Do you understand what I'm saying? Are you up for it?'

Manju did not hesitate. 'Ready, guruji.'

Gajendra said he knew it was crazy. He was full of fear. He knew the chances were that neither of them would survive. But they had to try. It was a matter of honour. They could not leave Yubraj helpless and wounded out there. And if they died in the rescue attempt, that was the price they both decided it was worth paying.

'We waited a few seconds,' Gajendra said. 'Counted down three, two, one. Grabbed our weapons and ran. Ran zigzagging across the field. Enemy bullets everywhere, kicking up the sand all around us. We were really pumped up. It was a miracle we did not get hit. But we make it to Yubraj. And he was unconscious. I thought he was just in shock.

'"Yubraj guruji," I shouted. "Yubraj guruji." No response. I shook him. Nothing. Enemy fire was coming in. Dhan was still there, laying down covering fire for us. We needed to move fast. I picked up Yubraj's legs. Manju got his arms. God, he was heavy – I could not believe it!

'In training we practised extraction loads of times and it was pretty easy, carrying mates who were conscious. It was even a bit of a laugh. But on the battlefield with the bullets flying and the casualty's unconscious. That's a different thing. It did not help that we were knackered and thirsty. The poor guy weighed a ton. We were sweating like pigs.'

Gajendra and Manju managed to carry Yubraj about 40 m, with Dhan following. The ground dipped a bit at this point and offered a bit of cover. Not much but some. They put Yubraj down and took a breather. There was another 40 m to go to reach the cover of the compound. 'I had another go at trying to wake him up,' Gajendra said. 'He was out. The enemy fire was too close for comfort. We got in the prone position. But I knew we had to keep moving. I told Dhan to give us cover. Me and Manju picked him up again and went for it.'

They reached the edge of the compound with enemy rounds still hitting the ground around them. Nearly there. A few seconds from safety! Then a complication no one could have foreseen. 'A bloody great dog!' Gajendra said. 'Snarling. Big teeth. Can you believe it? No way did it want us in that compound!

'We were in danger of getting shot in the back. And I knew the clock was ticking for Yubraj. He needed urgent medical attention. I shouted at the dog. I chucked stones at it. The bastard stood his ground. Finally I pointed my rifle at it and was about to pull the trigger when it just ran away. So we get Yubraj inside the wall and lay him down in a safe place.

'I'm shouting at him again. "Yubraj guruji, Yubraj guruji!" But he does not respond. Now I'm getting seriously worried. The whole section is bending over him. There's a battle going on all around us but we do not even notice it. We check for blood. I open his clothing. First the top. No blood, no bullet wounds. Not that we can see. We take off his trousers. There's a bit of a mark in the upper pelvis area on the left side. But it's more like a pencil mark. I thought it was a graze and not a bullet hole.

'I splashed a bit of cold water on his face and torso, try-ing to get him to wake up. His eyelids flicker. He opens his eyes. He says, "Morphine. Give me morphine." We were just so pleased to hear his voice.'

Every soldier carries a morphine auto-injector for reliev-ing the pain of battlefield casualties. Gajendra did not get the chance to administer it because at that moment the medical evacuation team arrived to take over the supervision of Yubraj. The last that Gajendra saw of him, he had slipped back into unconsciousness. But Gajendra felt reassured that he was in the best possible hands.

The fierce battle continued for several more hours. In the middle of the fighting word got passed around that Yubraj had not made it. His body had been recovered to Camp Bastion. 'Total shock when we found out,' Gajendra said. 'We were all mad as hell. We wanted revenge. We wanted to go in. Search door to door, find the bastards who did it. Take them out. Use our khukuris on them.' He shook his head.

At the end of a day and night of intense fighting the 2 RGR Battle Group returned to base with their heads held high but with heavy hearts. They had pushed the Taliban back from southern areas of Musa Qala, cleared ten compounds where the enemy had been holed up and recovered several caches of weapons and explosives. But they had lost a brother.

Two days later the MoD published an official notice of Yubraj's death. In it 2 RGR's CO, Lt Col Darby, said: 'Yubraj was a proud Nepali, a proud soldier and was exceptional-ly proud of being a Gurkha Rifleman. He knew the dangers involved in becoming a soldier and understood better than most what it meant to go to war; this was one of his greatest strengths. He died doing what he did best, amongst his greatest friends and admirers and for a cause he had taken the time to understand. He was brave, strong, hard and noble; he epitomized all that makes the Gurkhas great – the best. I was proud to have known him; he will not be forgotten.'

When Gajendra told me the story of how Yubraj died he did not make a big deal of his own role, and the bravery shown by Dhan and Manju. But make no mistake – what they did was truly heroic. The Platoon Commander, 2nd Lt Cochrane, was there on the ground and saw it all happen. In press interviews afterwards he said, 'The boys acted with immense bravery and with disregard for their own lives as they moved through open ground under fire to recover the casualty.'

This was no consolation to Gajendra, After he had finished telling me the story we were both in tears. Then an anger welled up in me. I was choked. I could not speak. I saluted my brave bother and we went our separate ways. The next morning I collected the re-supplies and returned to FOB Delhi by helicopter. A few days later we received orders to deploy south of Garmsir for a clear and search operation.

Of course, Yubraj was still on my mind. When you lose someone in those circumstances – a dear friend especially – it shakes you up. It makes you wonder if you might be next.

CHAPTER 11

MISSIONS OF MERCY

I learned fast about the brutalities of life. My first active deployment as a soldier of the British Army was to Sierra Leone, West Africa, in 2001. We were sent to train government forces and provide security in the capital, Freetown. At that time the country was coming to the end of a bitter civil war. Over the previous decade a rebel army called the Revolutionary United Front (RUF) and a smaller group of insurgents known as the West Side Boys had killed many thousands of civilians and government troops, and committed many atrocities. The previous year a patrol of British soldiers had been taken prisoner by the West Side Boys before being freed in a daring dawn assault by the Special Air Service (SAS).

By the time of our deployment, as a British Force alongside the United Nations Mission in Sierra Leone (UNMISL), the situation in the country was tense but improving. On a day of extreme heat we were returning to base after conducting a routine patrol. There were seven of us in two WMIKs. I was on the top of the front vehicle operating the GPMG. We were driving as fast as we could when I saw that the road ahead was covered in a cloud of dust. Some kind of incident had obviously occurred, but it was impossible to see what.

The dust was so thick that we had to slow right down. And as we got nearer to the incident I heard screams. The voices of women and children in extreme pain and fear. My first thought was this was an action by the RUF, who were notorious for their extreme brutality. They had mutilated many people by cutting off their limbs with machetes.

We were now at crawling speed. I loaded a live round in the chamber of the GPMG and swung it from right to left, ready for an attack from any direction. Ahead I could see figures moving through the swirls of dust. The screaming was getting louder. Then we reached the site. It was a scene of utter carnage.

In rural Sierra Leone people travelled about mainly in the backs of trucks that operated like buses. One of these trucks had come off the road and ended upside down in a deep ditch. All the passengers in the back had been thrown out. Dead and dying people, most of them women and children, lay about on the road crying and screaming in pain. A plume of smoke came from the engine of the truck. It looked as if it could explode at any second.

We had no way of knowing what had caused the accident. Maybe the driver had fallen asleep or maybe they had been ambushed by rebels. My initial reaction was to just stare hopelessly. I was the youngest member of the patrol. I had never seen anything like this. People were covered in blood. There was blood all over the road.

The Patrol Commander, Cpl Ram Rai, who was in the front vehicle with me, yelled at us to offer help. We got down from the WMIKs and walked among the injured and dying, offering our water bottles, using our field dressings on the wounds and providing the first aid we had learned. Some of the people who had been screaming or calling fell silent, and I was not sure whether they were unconscious or dead.

One woman had a badly injured baby daughter who was crying. She lay on the ground trying to pick up the baby and begging for help. The baby stopped crying and became unresponsive. I tried to give her water but it made no difference. Her mother watched helplessly. All around us people were losing the battle for life. Futures and dreams were dying in front of our eyes. In the split second it took for the truck to overturn, so many lives were changed or ended forever. It was a shock and a lesson for me, that the world could be this cruel to the innocent and defenceless.

As my team did what we could two small trucks arrived at high speed. They were from the local village and had come to help. They reacted like us at first – with disbelief and horror. Some recognized their loved ones and rushed to them. Others sobbed over dead bodies. Then soldiers and civilians worked together to save who we could.

The first thing we did was triage the victims – prioritize who should get treatment first. The dead we lifted to one side. The ones with minor injuries we left for their relatives to find and tend. We put the ones who were critically injured and in need of immediate medical attention into the local vehicles so they could be taken to hospital. These small trucks quickly filled up and we were asked if we could carry some of the injured in our WMIK.

Our Patrol Commander agreed. We took two critically injured middle-aged women and a little girl of about four, and set off for the hospital in Freetown. The women had leg fractures and, probably, internal injuries. The baby had no visible injuries but was unconscious. I held her in my arms. The two women were packed tightly together on the floor. Their eyes were opening and closing, but when they were open, they were staring up at me and the child. Their eyes were filled with tears. They looked terrified and in pain. Neither spoke. I wanted to say something to them and eventually came out with, 'How are you?'

They did not respond. It looked to me like they would not make it unless we got them to the hospital in the next few minutes. The child in my arms had her eyes closed and was breathing rapidly. I realized that one of the women was looking at her in particular. Was it her daughter? Or was she just reacting with maternal instinct? 'Is she yours?' I asked her.

There was no reaction. She lay there as if all the fight had gone out of her. I nodded at the other woman and looked down at the unconscious child, as if to say, 'Maybe she is your daughter?' No reaction from her either.

Perhaps the little girl belonged to neither. Perhaps her mother was one of the dead we had left back on the road. If she survived, she would grow up an orphan. I wondered whether I was really helping her, saving her life just so she could be alone and defenceless in this lawless country where women and children had been raped and mutilated.

The two women and child were getting worse in front of my eyes. They needed expert medical intervention as soon as possible if they were to survive. It was frustrating because Freetown was only a few miles away but we could not drive fast due to the terrible road, which was covered in potholes.

At one point the little girl had opened her eyes and that gave me hope. But they had been closed for a long time now and she was having breathing problems. There was no blood visible on her body or clothing, but it was likely she was bleeding internally. I touched her chest gently and could feel the struggle her lungs were making.

At that time I was a young, single man, but with plans to marry soon and have children. How would I feel if this were my daughter? My heart would be breaking. I knew I had to do everything possible to help her. It seemed to me very important that we find out whom the little girl belonged to so we could tell the staff at the hospital. If her mother or father had died in the crash then they needed to know about her extended family, who may be in another part of the country. Otherwise she could easily get lost in the system and be separated from her loved ones forever.

The key to this was the two critically ill women on the

floor of the WMIK in front of me. One of them opened her eyes and looked at the little girl again. And again I said, 'Is she yours? Is she yours?' This time the woman reacted, making a hand gesture that I took to mean she did not understand what I was saying.

Then she made a drinking gesture and pointed at the little girl. She was telling me to give her more water. I tilted my water bottle to the girl's lips and just managed to wet them. The woman on the floor pointed at the girl again and this time put her hand on her heart. A universal language. This was her daughter.

It was such a relief to know this. The show of motherly love, even as the woman was fighting to stay alive, was so touching. Of course, it made me think of my own mother. Of mothers the world over and how powerful the maternal instinct is for sacrifice and protection.

We were in such a terrible situation, one that I hoped never to go through again. Yet in the middle of it was this tender and moving moment. Tears came to my eyes. I looked away from the woman and out of the window, at the crowds of cars, motorbikes and people that were getting thicker as we approached Freetown.

'Kailash! Everything alright in the back there?' It was the Patrol Commander from the front seat.

'It's looking critical, guruji,' I replied. 'We need to get there soon.'

I looked back at the mother on the floor. Her eyes locked on mine. She saw my tears. It was as if she understood what

I had said. Her eyes kept closing as she drifted into unconsciousness. Then she would open them again, desperate to
keep fighting.

Her daughter's eyes had been closed for some time now.
Her breathing continued shallow and rapid. I feared she could
be dying in my arms. Her mother started to cry and tried to
lean forward to touch her child. But she was too weak to move
properly. She opened her mouth as if to speak but no sound
came out. The other woman was motionless.

Then the mother's body shook for a second or two and
white foam came out of her mouth. I had no idea what this
was but my immediate concern was that it might block her
breathing. I leaned forward and wiped the foam from her lips
with a cloth. Then I tried to give her water but she was too
weak to drink. She was trying to speak but hardly able to open
her mouth. Just a murmur, a whisper, that made no sense to
me. Then she slumped back; she continued to breathe.

This felt like the longest journey I had ever been on. It
took us an hour to reach the outskirts of Freetown. We had
been to the hospital before and knew the route well. But the
roads were getting more and more clogged with cars, motorbikes and people. Horns were honking all around us. Nobody
would give way or let us through even though we were trying
to tell them that we had casualties on board.

I was constantly checking that the child was OK. I shook
her hand. I touched her fingers. She did not react. I had a
good knowledge of life-saving techniques on the battlefield
and was able to feel the girl's pulse. It seemed fairly strong to

me but what did I know? I prayed for us to reach the hospital as soon as possible so I could hand her over to doctors.

The girl's mother woke up again. She pointed at her chest and tried to speak. I thought she was saying that she had been injured there. That was where her pain was. It made sense as there were no external signs of injury. When the truck rolled, she had received a big blow to the chest. And maybe that was the cause of the white foam. The other woman seemed in an even worse state. She had not moved or opened her eyes for a long time.

We finally made it to the hospital. We had radioed ahead and there was an emergency team of doctors and nurses on hand to receive the casualties. I jumped from the WMIK with the girl in my arms and placed her carefully on a waiting stretcher.

I was desperate for her to show some sign of recovery before I left her. If she would just open her eyes then I could wave her goodbye, and leave believing that she stood at least a chance of surviving. But the orderlies were already carrying her off and she was motionless on the stretcher. I watched her go. And just as I was about to turn away the miracle happened. The little girl opened one eye and looked at me. I waved, I smiled. I took it as a sign.

Meanwhile, the girl's mother and the other woman were also being taken away for treatment. Both were conscious now. The mother looked at me with tears in her eyes. She was trying to speak. She probably wanted to thank me. She gave up and raised a hand instead. I raised mine too. I said, 'Goodbye, and take care on the rest of your journey.'

Shortly after this incident our tour of Sierra Leone was complete and we returned to our base in Brunei, South-East Asia. We never did find out what happened to the little girl and the women we rescued from the bus crash. But the memory of that day stayed with us. The carnage we saw was as bad as anything I would encounter on the battlefield. The desperate dash to the hospital in the WMIK was one of the most nerve-racking journeys I had ever made. I do still think about that little girl. I believe she pulled through and I often wonder where she is and what became of her.

The British army base in Brunei is the only permanent British military presence in the Far East since Hong Kong was handed back to the Chinese in 1997. One of the two battalions of the Royal Gurkha Rifles is permanently stationed there, ready for immediate deployment in South-East Asia.

Our training routine in Brunei consisted of practising jungle warfare deep in the wild rainforests. I loved those jungle exercises. They lasted several days and you really felt you had changed and developed by the end.

On the first day of every such exercise, my body ached all over with the physical exertion required to hack through jungle in extreme heat and humidity. The second day could be even worse. But on day three something happened. I felt part of the jungle, as if I had merged with nature. All my senses were finely tuned to the sights, sounds and smells of the rainforest. I felt intensely happy.

My favourite part of the day was always the evening, when my body was pleasantly tired from moving from one ridge line to another, through dense undergrowth, or walking through swampland. The simple tasks of making camp, cooking and eating our army rations – usually mixed with noodles to give them extra flavour – were pure joy. And then we fell into our hammocks, craving sleep. It usually rained in the night but we would rig up a shelter. Listening to the rain and the sound of the insects I felt at peace with the world.

Shortly after returning from Sierra Leone we were sent on a day-long individual navigation exercise. The ability to navigate accurately is crucial in jungle conditions, when it is frequently impossible to see more than a few feet in any direction due to the density of the undergrowth. The point of the exercise was to navigate a route through a series of checkpoints, using the map coordinates I had been given, and I was expecting to complete the course and be back at base by early evening. We were fully briefed on safety measures, of course, in case anyone became lost or injured.

Sure enough I made good progress and was not far from base when I reached the edge of a swamp about 45 m across. I needed to get to the other side. There were no obvious crossing points but I had learned not to panic in these situations. I sat down on the edge of the swamp and considered the options.

If I did not find a way across I would have to retrace my steps and take another route back to base, even though it'd be getting dark soon. It would take too long and I would almost certainly get lost without light. I had no way of knowing how deep the water was in the swamp, or how thick and treacherous the mud on the bottom. If I tried to wade through I could easily get stuck or be sucked under.

I could just sit it out – wait till sunrise the next morning and take the long route back. But I had no food, nothing to sleep in and nothing to protect me. I would be vulnerable to poisonous snakes, crocodiles, leeches, hornets, scorpions and mosquitoes. No thanks.

I decided to go for the swamp crossing. No time to lose. I lifted my rifle high with my right arm and set off. The water was shallow and there were raised areas where the mud was more solid. I could feel it sinking a little beneath my steps but I made good progress. At a point just 20 m from the other side I started to relax.

The way I was stepping forward, trying to make myself as light as possible, reminded me of my sister, Gudiya, back in Nepal. When she was hunting for birds or small animals in the forest she was as light-footed as a tiger. I was laughing to myself at this memory, reminding myself to tell Gudiya about crossing the swamp the next time I saw her, when I suddenly lost my footing.

I took a step and my foot sank deep in the mud and got stuck. Trying to rebalance I brought my other foot forward but that got stuck, too. Then I realized my feet were not just stuck. The mud was pulling them down. I was being sucked in. In just a few seconds I had sunk up to my knees.

The thing not to do in this situation is panic. Any excessive movement just makes it worse … and I panicked. I tried to wriggle my feet. I bent down and tried to lift my legs with my hands. I put all my strength in to it. I heaved as hard as I could. My legs sunk deeper. I lost all reason at this point. I was covered in sweat and terrified I was about to drown in mud. I had no idea how to escape.

Now the mud was up to my waist. The webbing at the back of my uniform seemed to be keeping me upright and slowing down the sinking process. But that just meant my death would be even more lingering and agonizing unless I came up with a solution now, in the next couple of minutes. I told myself to keep calm and stop thrashing about.

But . . . the pressure of the mud pressing on my torso was now really hurting. I felt I was being squeezed by a giant fist. Breathing was becoming difficult. Maybe this was how I would die, not by drowning but by having the life literally squeezed out of me.

My mind went back to my childhood in Nepal. My mother and all the love she gave me. Her wonderful food. Working in the fields with all the family members. My little sister who hunted like a tiger. How I would pinch her behind Mum's back when she did anything naughty, and she would tell on me and Mum would not believe I had pinched her. I felt bad about that now. I promised myself that if I got through this I would treat Gudiya with love and respect from now on.

This was the first time as a soldier that I thought I was about to die. And I was not even in a combat zone, just a training exercise that had gone wrong due to my own poor decision. There would be several more occasions, especially in Afghanistan. I have already written about some of them in this book. But in such life-or-death moments my thoughts always went back to my family. And in particular what they would do without me. I was the only son. Each month the money I sent home helped to run the family home.

When I thought about this responsibility I knew that I could not die. I had to live. And it gave me the strength and determination to keep fighting. I reckoned I was now probably no more than 300 m from our training base at the harbour. That made it sound very close but in dense jungle, with vegetation so thick you could hardly see 20 m ahead, it seemed like a world away. Still, maybe one of my brothers would hear me if I shouted.

I filled my lungs and lifted my head, 'Guruji! Guruji! Can anyone hear me?' The only sound that came back was the hum of insects. Now a new terror struck me. Crocodiles. Or snakes. The swamplands were full of them. I was a ready meal on a plate for a hungry croc or snake. My imagination played tricks. I thought I felt movement in the water. I was panicking again.

An SOP in such a critical situation is to blow the whistle we are all equipped with. The whistle was located on the top left of my webbing. I grabbed it and blew a long blast that echoed through the thick jungle canopy. There was no answer. Night was beginning to fall now and the mud was inching up towards my chest. I was exhausted and desperately thirsty, but my water bottle was in the webbing on my back and it was impossible to reach.

Then out of desperation I tried something else. I leant my body forward and pushed back with one leg. Instantly that foot felt freer. I kept pushing. Was I imagining it or did the other foot also feel freer? I kept pushing, moving backwards and forwards now. I felt the mud giving me up. My body was rising in the water. The more of my legs I freed, the stronger I felt.

This gave me renewed hope. Suddenly I felt as strong as Superman. There was a raised patch of ground ahead of me. I dragged myself towards it, grabbed it, hauled most my body out of the water and mud. For a minute or so I just lay there, getting my breath back, thanking God for the extra strength he had given me at the vital moment.

But I was not safe yet. I still had 5 m of swamp to cross to get to the safety of the far side, and darkness was falling fast. I took it as carefully as I could, testing each step, expecting at any second to get sucked back down into the mud. But I made it. I lay down on hard ground, overcome with exhaustion and emotion. I twisted round to reach my water bottle and drank it all in a couple of gulps.

Ahead of me was a steep hill. I climbed it cautiously, aware of the dangers that lurked in the darkness. Beyond it I spotted the lights of the camp. What a sight for sore eyes! Finding new energy from somewhere I ran the rest of the way. All the time I had a smile on my face, thinking about my brothers and how they were going to tease me for getting stuck.

When I reached camp the rest of the company were all equipped with night lights and getting ready to go out into the jungle to search for me. They were relieved to see me, but it wasn't long before they were making 'hilarious' jokes about

ABOVE The vehicle patrol takes a quick break in the desert during Herrick IX, 2009.

BELOW Another foot patrol, this time to dominate the ground south of FOB Delhi in 2009. A local boy sits with me, with a poppy field in the background.

In 2016 my mother and father visited the UK for the first time and we tried to show them as much as we could. Above, in beautiful North Yorkshire and below in a very gloomy Trafalgar Square, London.

ABOVE During a Company exercise, practising our jungle skills in Brunei, 2018.

LEFT Outside my home in Brunei. Our Army base there is the only British military presence in the Far East.

LEFT   On leave at my house in Charali. My grandfather (seated, middle) is holding Anish, flanked by my father and mother (holding Alisa). Standing from the left are my sister Gudiya, my aunt, me and Sumitra.

BELOW   In 2018 I visited the National Memorial Arboretum in Staffordshire, a centre of remembrance for those who have served their country.

ABOVE With my family during the Dashain Festival in 2018.

RIGHT With my wife Sumitra and our children at their school in 2019.

ABOVE Another proud moment. After the publication of my first book, in 2019 I received an award from the International Nepalese Academy.

LEFT In RGR Officers' mess kit during the boxing night at the Infantry Training Centre at Catterick, 2019.

the soldier who got lost in the jungle and was never seen again! More seriously, it turned out that no one else had attempted to cross the swamp and from then on it was marked on the map as a place to be avoided.

It was not all exercises and drills in Brunei. We had time off and one Saturday I suggested to my Gurkha brother, Rfn Kusal, that we hire a car and do some exploring. So far all we had seen of Brunei was our base and the jungle. The country is a sovereign state on the north coast of the island of Borneo, surrounded by the Malaysian state of Sarawak. It may be tiny but it has lots to see, including the huge Jerudong Amusement Park, beautiful beaches and pristine rainforest.

With me behind the wheel and Kusal reading the map we spent a day exploring. In the early evening we decided to head for the capital, Bandar Seri Begawan. We were on a country road and approaching the main highway that would take us to the capital when we came across a motorcycle lying in the middle of the road. I slowed right down for a better look. There was no sign of the rider.

'How did that end up there?' Kusal said.

A good question. 'Maybe he stopped to go to the toilet,' I said. I pointed at the jungle, which came right down to the roadside. 'He's probably in there somewhere.' But that did not really make sense and I knew it. You would not just abandon your motorbike in the middle of the road, however desperate you were.

I stopped the car at the side of the road near the abandoned bike and switched on the hazard lights. We both got out of the car and approached the bike cautiously. My eyes scanned the surrounding trees and hills. Something did not feel quite right. I felt nervous but did not want to admit that to Kusal.

As in Nepal there is still widespread belief in ghosts on the island of Borneo. In camp in the evenings some of the senior guruji would tell tales of ghosts that made noises like humans crying. These ghosts would sneak into camp while we slept and cut one end of a person's hammock so he fell to the ground with a bad bump. Or they made soldiers on jungle exercise lose their bearings and their minds, so they wandered lost for days on end. That really made me wonder about my experience in the swamp!

Well, the motorbike was certainly real. We bent down and inspected it. The frame was dented. It looked like it had been in an accident. It was almost dark by now. As we stood there wondering what to do a car approached at high speed from the main highway with headlights on full beam.

The headlights lit up the figure of a man lying in the road about 100 m from us. Near the man was a stationary car with people inside. The speeding car missed the body in the road and the stationary car, and shot past us. As we ran towards the man in the road I painted a quick picture in my head of what I thought had happened.

The car that was now parked had collided with the motorbike. The bike rider had been knocked flying. The bike had continued sliding down the road before finally toppling on its side.

The man in the road did not respond when we reached him. We carried him to the side, out of the way of speeding vehicles. I told Kusal to tell the driver of the parked car to move it as it was in a dangerous position. Meanwhile, I ran back to our vehicle and drove it up so its headlights shone on the injured man.

The other car now moved to the side of the road, out of harm's way. Kusal returned and said there was a family inside and they had confirmed my theory of what had happened. They were unharmed but in a state of shock. Kusal and I worked on the injured motorbike rider. I removed his helmet and loosened his clothes. He did not respond to our questions. I checked his pulse but could not feel anything. His eyes were closed.

I decided to perform CPR (Cardiopulmonary Resuscitation) to get his heart beating again, and was just about to start when he moved and his eyelids flickered. He began to sweat profusely. At that moment we heard the wail of sirens and within a minute police and ambulance teams had arrived, blue lights flashing in the dark.

The police went over to the family in the car and the paramedics dealt with the injured man. He was now fully conscious and looking around with a puzzled expression. Perhaps he was confused to see two Gurkhas staring back at him! They lifted him onto a stretcher and, as they slid him into the back of the ambulance, he looked straight into my eyes. There were no words. There was no need. We each lifted a hand in farewell and then the doors were closed.

The next day I wrote a letter to my parents in Nepal telling them all about my life in Brunei. Except I did not tell them everything. I did not mention the navigation exercise that went wrong and the close shave in the swamp, and I did not mention finding the injured motorbike rider. I did not want to tell them anything that would make them worry. And years later, when I was serving in Afghanistan, it was the same. I always tried to protect them from the dangerous side of life, even if I could not always protect myself.

CHAPTER 12

MORE SHATTERING NEWS

I was leading my patrol in a battle zone when we came across a group of enemy fighters that hugely outnumbered us. We turned to escape and they followed us, through a field with a line of trees on one side. Beyond the field was a water channel. We jumped into it and ran fast down the middle.

My heart was pumping, I was breathing rapidly. We were all exhausted and thirsty. I wondered if I could somehow drink the water from the channel as I ran along. The enemy did not jump in the channel after us; they were shooting from above. The bullets were splashing in the water around us and the enemy's voices were getting louder. They were closing in.

We decided to turn and return fire but our ammunition ran out. Then the enemy fighters were standing right over us. One of them jumped in the channel next to me and pressed the barrel of his gun to my forehead. I put my hand on my khukuri knife. I was going to slash his throat before he pulled the trigger.

Then I woke up. I was in my cot bed in a temporary Observation Post (OP) in the desert, about 4 km north-west of FOB Delhi. There were twelve of us altogether – seven Gurkhas and five from the ANP (Afghan National Police) and our job was to monitor, disrupt and give warning of any insurgent threats towards FOB Delhi and Garmsir District Centre where our Company and Battle Group Headquarters were located.

I was covered in sweat and felt dizzy. When I think back on it I reckon I was still grieving for Yubraj, who had been killed less than two weeks earlier. When I sat up I almost vomited. I sat on the edge of the cot bed and drank half of the water in my bottle. My cot was just outside a makeshift sleeping area made by blocks of Hesco – giant hessian and wire sacks filled with earth and stone – where the rest of my section was sleeping. (The reason for me sleeping apart from my bhaiharu, by the way, is that my snoring is legendary – someone once said it was like a train coming down the tracks at you!)

It was exactly 0030 hours. Inside the sleeping area my brothers were also snoring like hell. There was a thin moon, but it was enough to cast light and shadows. The OP was on a hill and at the top, about 75 m high, was a *sangar* (sentry post). I called up to my two bhaiharu on duty there. They waved back.

The nightmare was still with me. I wiped the sweat from my face with a rag and lay back, recalling the moment when the enemy fighter pressed the barrel of his gun to my forehead. I told myself to calm down. I was a highly trained professional. I would never allow myself to get in that situation. Besides, I had my lucky coin.

Still, I checked that my weapon was within reach as I lay in bed. Then I pulled the hood of my sleeping bag over my head and tried to go back to sleep. There was a breeze that cooled my cheeks and always those barking dogs in a distant village. I was reminded of my childhood.

Sleep would not come so I opened my eyes and looked up at the stars. It was a perfectly clear sky. The white band of the Milky Way was clearly visible. I spotted a shooting star. Then another. After a while, once my eyes adjusted, I was seeing them every few seconds. Each time I said a little prayer for the wealth and wellbeing of my family.

That set me thinking about home in the UK. I decided that when I returned from this tour of duty I would take the family on a long drive somewhere – maybe to Durdle Door, by the sea, in Dorset. I had never been there. There was so much of England for us still to explore. But I had heard that it was a lovely place. Then I would be able to give them all the love and attention that I was not able to, while I was on duty so far away.

Eventually I drifted off. Then voices from the sangar, 'Guruji! Guruji!' I thought it was another dream. I turned over

and tried to burrow deeper in to the cot. But the voices continued. I opened my eyes and this time, instead of shooting stars,
I saw tracer rounds flying across the sky. Were they friendly or
enemy? Stupid question. There were no friendly forces nearby.

A few seconds later came the sound of heavy gunfire. I sat
up and yelled at the sentries on top of the hill, 'What the hell's
happening?' As I did so I fell out of my cot bed onto the hard
desert ground. The gunfire continued. My brothers inside the
sleeping area still had not reacted.

Following the tracer rounds I could see that they were striking the top of the hill. We were coming under attack. 'Stand
to, stand to!' I screamed. The tracers and gunfire were now
coming in non-stop. I was struggling to put on my Osprey
body armour. I shouted up at the sentries in the sangar, 'You
OK up there?' They did not reply.

Neither did my brothers behind the Hesco blocks. I could
not find my boots so I rushed in to the sleeping area without
them. 'Bhaiharu, I shouted stand to!' I screamed. Now they
got the message. As they hurried to get dressed and grab their
weapons I went back to look for my footwear.

It was 0330 hours, still dark but with just enough moon-
light to make out shapes. I was seriously worried about my two
bhaiharu on the top of the hill. They had not replied when I
shouted up at them and they were not returning the enemy's
fire.

There could be an explanation for that. They could be
searching for an exact location before opening fire. Or they
could have been hit. They could be lying up there dead. Or

badly injured and in need of emergency treatment. I needed to find out. There was no time to find my boots. I grabbed my weapon and started climbing the hill.

It was hard going, walking over rough desert ground in stockinged feet, but every second could be precious. I ignored the pain and carried on. As I climbed I was looking out for the ANP. I could not see any, which was worrying. These guys were, frankly, in my view not to be fully trusted.

When I was fighting at Now Zad in 2006 there were a number of ALP (Afghan Local Police) attached to us in our FOB. During one battle they supplied the enemy with the co-ordinates so they could attack our safe house. When we discovered this we detained and disarmed them.

What we really wanted to do was kill them, but under the ROE we had to let them go. Our Commanding Officer sent them back to their headquarters, but who knew if they got there? They probably joined the Taliban instead. Now my fear was that the ANP attached to our OP had helped the insurgents attack the sentries on duty, or even kidnap them.

I was climbing the hill as fast as I could, following the path we had made to the sangar at the top. I did not want to use the torch as it would be a big invitation for enemy snipers, so I had to tread carefully in the dark. The rest of my section were about 40 m behind me. I could hear their breathing coming fast and loud. Then the bullets were flying above our heads. Some were striking the fortified sangar at the top.

When I reached the top I still had to cross about 30 m of open, uneven ground to reach the sangar on the far edge of the hill. My heart was racing as I ran across. 'Bhaiharu, bhai-haru!' There was no answer from the sangar. I was just 5 m away and still there was no sign of them. Then I spotted them, outside the sentry post on the right-hand side. They had taken a lighter GPMG from inside and were preparing to fire at the Taliban, one holding the ammunition belt while the other took aim.

I knelt down next to them. 'You alright?'

'Yes, no problem, guruji.' The enemy had stopped firing for now while my men pointed the GPMG roughly where we thought the enemy were. It was impossible to make anything out as it was still dark. But I was just relieved they were OK. Then the firing started again. I crouched against the wall of the sangar and shouted, 'Take cover, take cover!' I got my rifle ready to engage.

The rest of the section were now on the top of the hill. They too were shouting 'Take cover!' They flattened themselves on the stony ground, then started to crawl towards the sangar. I worked out the enemy position from the tracer rounds coming towards us. The guys on the GPMG fired back and so did I. I grabbed the radio handset and sent a message to our Company Ops Room in FOB Delhi. 'O this is 32C. Contact. Wait out.'

By this time the rest of the unit had reached the sangar on their bellies. They were under the command of Nagen, one of the best 2ICs I ever had. 'OK, listen up, bhaiharu,' I said. 'The enemy are directly to the front. Two hundred and fifty metres.' Their bullets were skimming our heads as I spoke. I ordered my men to return rapid fire.

We had far greater firepower than the enemy: a GMG, GPMG and Minimi machine gun, as well as our assault rifles. The GMG especially is a real beast, producing massive firepower and deafening noise.

Then earsplitting noise, pumping adrenaline. 'I'm going to kill you!' Rabin yelled.

'Kill the bastards!' Raju shouted.

Nagen tried to keep things calm. 'Aim, shoot. Aim, shoot, OK. Control the gun.'

Then he said, '*Schermuly, Schermuly*' – meaning he was about to send up a parachute illumination flare. Followed by, 'Stand by, stand by.'

He launched a flare that hung in the air for 40 seconds, lighting up the ground in front of us for several metres. We scanned the area. A cluster of buildings about 250 m away, the Helmand River flowing between the buildings and our OP. At the corner of one of the buildings a man moved. He began to shoot at us. 'Enemy, enemy!' I shouted.

I engaged with my rifle. The rest of the section opened up with their weapons. The Schermuly light was fading. Our tracer rounds looked like they were hitting the target but the enemy fighter was still firing back – we could see the muzzle flash. My 2IC fired another flare up and we spent another 40 seconds scanning the lit-up landscape. We spotted no more enemy fighters but they kept firing at us. A few seconds later the Taliban we had spotted before appeared again, ran to the back of the building and took cover. It happened too quickly for us to take him down – a lucky escape for him.

At this point there was a bit of a lull in proceedings. I took the opportunity to grab the radio handset and send in a full contact report to HQ FOB Delhi. The voice that came on the other end belonged to our OC Sahib – Major J P Davies MBE, now Colonel of the Brigade of Gurkhas. Over several years I have built a huge respect for his calm and composed leadership. He is also the kindest officer I have ever worked with.

'Well done, Kailash,' he replied, adding that mortar cover, illum and a QRF (Quick Reaction Force) were on call. It was a great morale booster to hear such words from Major Davies.

We were on top by this point. After half an hour's engagement we had suppressed the enemy's fire. It made sense to push home the advantage but the darkness seemed thicker than ever, now that the flares had faded. There was still some time to go before dawn, and we decided to wait for the enemy's next move.

As we lay there by the sangar, I instructed Nagen to scan enemy territory using the Viper thermal night-vision system attached to his rifle sight. I did the same using my HMNVS. As we were looking the firing started up again. We returned fire on a massive scale. I could hear my men changing the magazines on their rifles.

Then someone yelled from the far end of the sangar 'GMG rounds, GMG rounds'. The GMG had run out of ammunition. Nagen and Rabin hurried to resupply it. A couple of minutes later it resumed heavy firing.

It was really hard to assess the enemy's strength. It could be that under cover of darkness they were advancing to attack us at close quarters. So I decided to call for a mortar illumination round, which is even brighter than the Schermuly flare. As it hung in the sky the insurgents stopped firing and we all scanned the terrain in front of us, hands firmly on our weapons, looking for enemy fighters.

Nothing. Then, about 250 m away, the group of three or four buildings that we had given the name 'Kathmandu 2'. Two men ran from one building to another. One appeared to have a weapon. They hid behind the second building.

'Enemy, enemy!' I shouted and pointed my rifle.

'Whereabouts, guruji?' Nagen said.

'Reference Kathmandu 2. Enemy withdrawing. Watch out.'

They escaped. The light from the mortar round faded, so we continued to wait and watch. I felt the sweat drying on my body. Soon I even felt a bit cold. Then I noticed that my feet were hurting – I had forgotten I was not wearing any boots! I said nothing about this to my team. It was not a good example to set. I was supposed to be in full fighting gear!

We relaxed a bit. The bhaiharu were whispering to each other. Nagen instructed us to refill the ammunition in our magazines, and feed new belts into the GMG and GPMG. I stood up and walked round, asking everyone if they were OK.

As I reached one side of the hill I spotted two other pax (i.e. unidentified people, could be insurgents) approaching from the bottom of the slope. Who the hell were they? What did they want? I was immediately scared and suspicious. One possible explanation was that they were suicide bombers. They saw me but carried on coming.

'Stop, stop, STOP!' I yelled.

Still they continued to approach. I shouted again and pointed the laser torch on the front of my weapon at them. They were wearing civilian clothes and carrying guns. Now they were just 20 m away. I moved my index finger onto the trigger. Nagen and Raju joined me. We were all yelling at them to stop and pointing our weapons.

This was too dangerous, I was about to pull the trigger when they stopped, raised their rifles above their heads with both hands and shouted, 'Police!' This did not make much sense to me. Why the hell would they be turning up now? Why had they not been here to help us when we were under fire? However, we searched them and checked their papers and they were indeed ANP.

As I speak some Urdu (because it is similar to Hindi, anyone who speaks Nepali can generally understand some of it) I asked them in their own language what they were doing. They answered that they were on routine patrol, which seemed odd as I had never known ANPs conduct patrols so early in the morning. It was possible that they had been helping the Taliban to target us. We had no way of knowing and we never did find out.

There followed a fifteen-minute stand-to in which we remained alert with weapons at the ready, but continued with routine tasks. Two bhaiharu stayed at the sangar on guard duty and the rest of us, including the ANPs, returned to the accommodation.

By this time it was about 0500 hours and the sun was

coming up. But it remained cold. We were all dead tired after the firefight. But before we grabbed some sleep we needed to make some battle preparations. My 2IC ordered everyone to clean and oil their weapons and make sure ammunition was ready to be used. While we did this he sorted out the duty rota.

Then we were free to sleep. I went out like a light. Two hours later I woke to bright sunshine. I made a mug of coffee and as we got ready for the day ahead we were all talking about the firefight in the dark. Then there were two loud explosions followed by a whistling sound.

'IDF,' I yelled and got down in the prone position, spilling that wonderful cup of coffee on the ground before I had even started to drink it. It looked like we were coming under mortar attack. If a shell landed on top of us that could mean the end for all of us. I closed my eyes and braced myself.

A few seconds later the next shell exploded harmlessly in the desert 100 m away. Maybe we were not being targeted after all. Big relief all round. We waited ten minutes in case of another IDF attack but it did not come. I told the bhaiharu on sentry duty to see if they could locate where the enemy were releasing the IDF, and we started to prepare our lunch.

There was another scare when a couple of bangs went off close by. We hit the deck as fast as we could. This definitely was not an IDF attack but I could not work out what had caused the bangs. I asked the sentries for an update. They had not been able to pinpoint where the IDF were fired from, though they reported that two ANPs were approaching our OP from the direction of the Helmand River.

The two men walked into the OP and greeted me in Urdu: 'How are you, commander?' One was carrying a bowl. He handed it to me. It was full of small fish from the river.

Even in the desert, in the middle of a combat zone, we must be polite to each other. I gave the man a hug and said, '*Dera manana*', meaning 'Thank you very much' in Pashto. Then I had an idea. 'How did you catch the fish?' I said.

'We threw a couple of grenades in the river,' he replied. Now I knew what the bangs had been.

That evening one of my bhaiharu cooked up the fish with some rice. It was the tastiest meal I ever had in the desert. The rest of the day had been uneventful and blisteringly hot. As we ate that delicious meal we were enjoying the cool evening air and feeling pretty relaxed.

But never too relaxed. We knew that the situation could change in a split second and that we had to be prepared and alert at all times. Before we went to bed Raju and I checked the Claymore mine outside our OP. The Claymore is a directional anti-personnel mine that can be detonated by remote control – a really effective defence if the enemy is attacking our position at close quarters.

However, it is easy to sabotage as anyone can turn it round so it is pointing back rather than forward. It even has a sign on it that says, 'Front toward enemy'! Sometimes the Taliban sent children to ask us for sweets or pens. While we were distracted, the kids would switch it round. So first thing in the morning and last thing at night we checked it was still pointing in the right direction.

The Claymore was good. When we had sorted out the rota for sentry duty we went to bed. Once more I lay there looking at the moon and stars, feeling the desert wind on my cheeks and thinking of my family. My two children were growing up fast. I really missed them – just the ordinary things, like family meals, taking them to school and collecting them.

When they saw the dads of other kids dropping them off at the school gates, did they resent me for not doing the same? Even when I was back at home I was often too busy to do the school run. They would say, 'It's your turn to pick us up today, Dad. Why does Mum always have to do it?' They were too young to understand. I comforted myself with the thought that it was only my body lying here in this desert wasteland. My heart was with them.

The following morning another section relieved us at the OP and we returned to FOB Delhi. It was another scorching day, and we were exhausted and thirsty when we got back. While we were rehydrating the CSM (Company Sergeant Major) Dhailindra KC ordered us to assemble in the briefing area next to our Ops Room. We were to form an O Group – a general meeting in which information and orders are given out.

It was late afternoon and the available men from the Company were gathering. This was unusual in itself. It probably meant that an important announcement was going to be made. This could be good or bad. My hope was that someone was being promoted. That was always a morale booster for all of us – there was not much to cheer about on a tour in Helmand Province.

The CSM, the Company Commander, Major Davies and his 2IC Capt Nanibabu Magar entered the briefing area together. They looked nervous. We were expectant. I think most of us reckoned it would be good news. The CSM told us to listen to 'OC Sahib'. I was studying his face for clues. He was expressionless. Then he began talking.

'I don't know how to say this. I am in no fit state to utter the words. But as your Officer Commanding it is my responsibility to inform you of what happened last night.'

You could have heard a pin drop.

'It is my sad duty to announce that in an IED strike yesterday in Musa Qala District we lost one of our best men. Our brother and friend, Colour Sergeant Krishna Bahadur Dura.'

The silence continued. Now it was the silence of disbelief. People were crying. Including me. People were holding their heads in their hands. I had had a special connection with Krishna guruji. We had been together many years. He had joined the British Army in 1992, seven years before me. This was his third tour of Afghanistan. We had laughed together and fought together. We had eaten out of the same mess tin. He was my inspiration, my role model. My teacher, my guruji.

I left the Ops Room and went to my cot. I sat down on the edge and thought about Krishna and his family. He had a wife and two children back in the UK. By now they would have had the news. All the plans they had for the future – torn up. The 'Welcome Home' card the kids were probably planning that would never be written or given. So much destroyed in a second.

Of course I was not just grieving for Krishna and his family. I was thinking about my numberi, Yubraj, whose recent death was still like an unhealed scar in my mind. I was also thinking of my own family. The pain and agony they would go through if anything happened to me. I needed to express what I felt. So I took out my battlefield notebook and started to write:

My dearest guruji,
You left us so abruptly. You taught us so many things.
Now all we have is our memories of you. But they will
last for as long as we live.

No matter who we are, or where we come from,
we have to leave this life one day. It is just a question
of when. You left us early. There were still so many
things we wanted to learn from you. You left many
lessons incomplete. But I believe that somewhere you
are waiting for us. And one day we will sit down
again and share food and drink as we once did.

You will always be with us and we will always be
with you.
Your dearest friend
Cpl Kailash bhai
2 RGR FOB Delhi

By the time I finished writing the tears were streaming down my face.

CHAPTER 13

GOING HOME

The loadmaster is yelling something. I cannot hear him over the roar of the C130's engines. Then the back doors close. We are strapped in, helmets on. We are going home, leaving the hell of Helmand Province behind for fourteen days' R&R back in the UK. But there is no sense of relief. Not yet. The Hercules taxis, turns and roars into the air. The pilot is not hanging about. Down below, Camp Bastion turns into a dusty dot. We climb steeply. Everyone is aware of the danger of enemy RPGs. One strike could take us down.

Once we are above 3,700 feet – the maximum enemy range – everyone relaxes. It is real! We're on our way home. We have survived another tour. The flight to RAF Brize Norton – via

Saudi Arabia or Bahrain, then Cyprus – seems to take forever. In that time we chat and catch up on sleep, but mostly we are lost in our private thoughts. This is how it used to go on those airlifts back to the UK.

Of course I would think about seeing my family again and get very excited about that. The kids would really have grown. My wife would be so pleased to have me back so we could share special times together. I would get to be a responsible husband and father, taking the kids to school, helping around the house. I always felt guilty about that – that being so far away I was not discharging my duties; then I would remind myself I was putting my life on the line for them every day. Above all I looked forward to that feeling of security and love I always get from my family.

Then my mind would drift back to what we all had just gone through. The ambushes we survived, the firefights we endured, the IEDs we narrowly avoided. The brothers we lost. We were turning our backs on all that, at least for now. It was not a good idea to dwell on it for too long and, at some point in the flight, I always cheered myself up by remembering the first flight I had ever taken, from Kathmandu to London Heathrow, in February 1999. That was when I had just passed the final selection board in Nepal for entry into the Brigade of Gurkhas and I was sitting next to my numberi, Yubraj.

As I wrote earlier, we were nervous, we were homesick and we could not believe how small the toilet on the plane was. By then we had received some basic instructions in Western ways – how to use a knife and fork, and the mysteries of a sit-down

WC! But we had little idea of what to expect when we landed.

All the way on the flight we kept taking turns to sit in the window seat so we could look down on the earth from a height even greater than Mount Everest. Then there were all the gadgets, like adjustable seats and individual TV screens (we struggled to use these, but just about got the hang of them as we were about to land). To us this was as thrilling as being in a space rocket.

The plane landed in darkness and I remember the thrill of seeing all the electric lights down below, spreading as far as you could see. When the plane reached the gate and finally stopped we did not know what to do. We just kept our eyes on our *gurujiharu*, the senior soldiers in charge of us. The other passengers, all civilians, disembarked first. Some of them welcomed us to the UK and wished us luck. Others looked at us a bit suspiciously as they walked down the plane. Then the gurujiharu gave us the signal to move.

We were fast-tracked through immigration. I remember more than anything how bright the lights were in the terminal building. My mum had told me that the lights in a big city like London would be so bright you would not be able to tell the difference between night and day. And I saw now that she was right. We seemed to be attracting a lot of attention from other passengers. The Gurkhas are famous, and we must have stood out in our smart travelling uniforms (some of us were wearing ties for the first time and had needed help putting them on). People were smiling and saying things that I could not understand. I just kept my eyes on the gurujharu and did what I was told.

After we had picked up our bags from the carousel we were shepherded out of the terminal building to waiting buses. This was my first experience of British weather! It was early in the morning in February and it was bitterly cold. I looked at my watch to see what time it was but there was just an empty wrist. I had given my watch to one of the unsuccessful candidates at the selection board in Pokhara – it was a tradition that the ones who passed gave a gift to the ones who failed. I wondered if the weather would get any warmer. It was just a short walk to the bus but the air was the coldest I had ever experienced.

The bus driver, who was English, said, '*Namaskar*' ('Hello') as I got on board, which made me feel at home straightaway. The engine was running, the heating was on. It was a brand-new, really smart vehicle. The seats were luxurious, the lights were bright, the windows were clean – so different from the rickety old buses I was used to in Nepal. Yubraj and I sat together again and waited for the final part of the journey.

In a way this was as exciting as the flight. The road network and infrastructure of a Western country is so different from a developing country like Nepal, and this was especially the case twenty years ago. We could not believe how smooth and well-built the roads were. There were road signs everywhere. And when we hit the M25 the number of the cars and the discipline of the driving, with everyone sticking to their lanes except when they overtook, was amazing.

The buses drove in convoy in the inside lane, giving us all time to stare out at the passing cars and vehicles. It was getting light by then but all the car lights were still on, a river of red lights up ahead and a river of white lights flowing towards us. At the side of the road the buildings were also lit up and beyond them I could see neat fields covered in snow. It had been a long journey from Kathmandu but I did not feel at all tired. Too much to take in.

Finally, we arrived at our home for the next nine months. Queen Elizabeth Barracks at Church Crookham near Fleet, Hampshire was a training base for the Gurkha regiments until the year 2000, when it was decommissioned and our base was moved to Shorncliffe Camp near Folkestone in Kent. My intake was the last-but-one to be based at Church Crookham. The camp was pretty standard – a series of wooden huts – but it was clean and well-organized, and I felt at home there.

Next to my bed I had a side table with a lamp on it. There was a tin cupboard to store our belongings and military kit. The showers were hot. The sit-down toilets took me a couple of days to get used to. What surprised and pleased me was the food, which was mostly Nepalese – daal, rice, pork and chicken curry. The only thing I did not like was baked beans for breakfast but I soon got used to them.

For the first few weeks we stayed on base getting fit and doing basic training in weapons, drill, fieldcraft and teamwork, the essentials for any combat infantryman. For us there was another element – cultural training. Our first exposure to the UK, apart from the day we arrived, came with a visit to Aldershot town centre with our guruji. We were impressed by the malls and all the different shops. The people were very friendly and respectful. They said hello, they said how smart we looked and told us how brave they knew the Gurkha soldiers were. Some even gave us priority and opened doors for us.

But what interested me more than anything was the different kinds of food on offer.

I was desperate to try KFC or a McDonald's burger. I had enough money on me but I was too shy to go inside. I did not know what to choose or how to order and I did not want to make a fool of myself, so I just stood outside and looked in. Also, I was worried about losing sight of our guruji. I did not want to be left stranded in the middle of Aldershot not knowing how to get back to barracks. Later I tried all the fast food and decided I liked KFC the best. Chinese food – ribs and rice – was also pretty good because it reminded me of home. But I have to say that my mum's, and now my wife's, cooking is still the best.

Aldershot was not too difficult to deal with. Our next experience was something else. As part of our cultural training we were taken to London. We travelled by train to Waterloo station, caught different tube trains and sat on the upper deck of on an open-top bus for a sightseeing tour, which took us past many famous sights including Buckingham Palace, the Houses of Parliament, London Bridge and the Tower of London.

Of course I had been to Kathmandu and, for a boy from a remote mountain village, that had seemed very big and crowded. But London was overwhelming. It was interesting to observe the people. So many seemed in a great hurry. They were on a mission and walked fast with their heads down. But others were strangers like us. They walked slowly and looked around, taking photographs. They looked as if they came from every country in the world.

I was also struck by the buildings – how many, how different they were, how clean, above all how big and tall. We used to say, when I was growing up, that if you went to a big city your *dhaka topi* (the traditional cap worn by Nepalese men) would fall off because you would always be leaning back so far to see the tops of the buildings. And now I found this was true. The building that really fascinated me was Tower Bridge. We were told that it could lift up to let big boats through and I willed it to happen while we were there. No such luck, but I loved watching the other boats on the river and wished I was on one. It was also fascinating to compare the powerful and wide Thames with the mountain rivers I knew from my childhood.

But if I had to name one thing that really sticks in my mind it's going on the London Underground. For a start I just could not get my head around the tube map. Our guruji stood our group of ten in front of a big map at the entrance of one of the stations, and tried to explain about the different lines and how they linked together. He then pointed out on the map where we were about to go, and told us to stick close to him and follow his instructions. That sounded easy enough but it did not work out that way.

I cannot remember now where we went exactly. But being underground frightened and confused me from the very beginning. As we went down the escalator, then waited for the train on the platform I kept my eyes glued to the guruji.

When we got on the train I calmed down a bit. There was room for us all to stand in a group and our guruji was keeping a close eye on us. But as the train went along it picked up more and more people at the different stations, and it was no longer possible to stand in one group.

Eventually, two of us got separated from the rest. I keep looking over the heads of the passengers to check they were still there and seeing our guruji looking calm. All we had to do was keep an eye on him and move when he made the signal. But even more passengers were getting on. Now it was not even possible to hold on to anything. When the train came into a station and stopped, I was in danger of overbalancing, and had to stop myself grabbing on to the nearest person.

Then we came into another station and there was complete chaos – people squeezing off the train, even more people squeezing on. Across the carriage I saw our guruji saying something and making signals. Then I lost sight of him and the rest of our numberi. When the train doors closed and the train set off again I saw that the group had gone. My colleague and I had been left behind! We looked at each other. What the hell should we do? Maybe they had moved further down the carriage. We strained to look but could not see them. We were sweating now, panicking. Lost in the big city! I could feel people staring at us, sensing something was wrong.

This all happened in a minute or less. Then I calmed down a bit and remembered the instructions our guruji had given us before we descended into the tube network. If any of us got separated from the main group we were to get off at the next stop on the line and wait. I reminded my friend and a few seconds later, when the doors of the train opened at the next station, we pushed our way through and disembarked. Then we stood there watching the world go by and wondering what would happen next.

We must have stood there for half an hour, just watching the faces – hundreds, thousands of them, of all creeds and colours. In all of them we looked anxiously for the face of our guruji. It was the longest half hour of my life. What would we do if he did not come? We felt helpless, like newborn babies. Then, just when we were losing hope, there he was, striding towards us, a huge grin on his face.

He was not angry at all. He said we had done the right thing. But he still made fun of us. And when we joined up again with the rest of the section there was lots of joking. Later, back in barracks, the whole platoon got to know about it and for a while we were famous as the Gurkhas who almost got lost forever on the London Underground.

These now seem such innocent days. Flying back to the UK for fourteen days' leave, with a combat tour or two of Afghanistan under my belt, I had plenty more frightening situations to look back on. But that memory of getting lost in London always brought a smile to my face and put me in a good mood for seeing my family again. The relief of being back with them, being at home in a completely relaxing environment, was pure joy. Seeing the cards the kids had made on the side table: 'Welcome home, Dad!' Holding my wife, Sumitra, and my children, Alisa and Anish, in my arms.

In our culture we do not express our emotions very openly. But Sumitra and I love each other deeply. As I stood there in the hallway with my kitbag, she would always whisper to me that the tour had seemed to go on forever, that she had counted the days and hours till I returned. And that meant the world to me. It made me realize I would do anything for her and the children – including giving up my own life.

Before I could really relax I had to call my other home, in Nepal, and tell my mum and dad I had arrived safely in the UK. They were always so relieved when I went home on leave. As their only son I was especially precious to them. Whenever I spoke to them or wrote to them from Afghanistan I tried to downplay the danger I was in. I never gave them any details of where we were, or told them about the close shaves I had or the bad things I saw. But they did not need telling. They knew how dangerous it was over there. Mum told me she prayed for me in the temple every day. So when I went back to the UK they could finally breathe a sigh of relief, knowing I was safe and happy for a couple of weeks at least.

Of course, Alisa and Anish always looked like giants compared to the last time I had seen them. They loved showing me their homework, very proud of how neat and serious it was. Alisa was good at drawing and showed me her drawings of elephants and birds, and different types of fruit trees. Then they got their toys out – Alisa's baby doll, Anish's gun. He ran around the sitting room making shooting noises: *'tatatatata ta ta.'*

Sumitra would cook me a special meal – maybe momos followed by pork curry – and then I had what was probably the greatest luxury of all. A big, comfortable bed and the knowledge that nothing would interrupt my sleep. No one trying to kill me. No pre-dawn start. No sentry to relieve. No needing to stay awake on sentry duty – and risking my life and everyone else's if I fell asleep for even one second. And no worry eating into my brain about the dangers of the following day and the lives of the men I was responsible for.

It made me realize that in Afghanistan you learn to op-erate without proper sleep. Here, at home, I made a pillow of my arms for Sumitra to rest her head on and closed my eyes in perfect happiness. Sometimes I would wake up in the middle of the night needing the toilet and forgetting for a split second where I was. I would tense up, thinking I was on the battlefield, trying to work it out. Then I would see the outline of the family photographs on the bedroom wall and relax. Deep breath. Get up, go quietly to the bathroom, come back to bed with my wife still blissfully asleep and take a sip of water from the glass on the bedside table. That, to me, was pure contentment.

In the mornings I had the pleasure of taking the kids to school. One either side of me they hung on to my arms, wide grins on their faces, proud to be showing me off to their friends and their teachers, and me so proud of them in return. I think they were a bit curious about me actually. They knew I was their dad but, still, I was away from home so much that I was also a little bit of a stranger to them.

They knew the time we had together was precious and they wanted to get to know me better. Anish wanted me to play with him on his Xbox or go out cycling with him. Alisa wanted me to buy her a pet so we got her two hamsters. They both asked me to get them sweets and chocolate whenever I went to the local Tesco. I had to be careful here. I loved giving them treats, but I did not want to spoil them or give them more than their friends had. Then it would be difficult for Sumitra to keep them happy when I went away again.

One of our favourite things to do was go to the local park while Sumitra stayed at home to cook us a wonderful meal. I loved being in the English outdoors, which was so different from Afghanistan. There it was desert. The sun beat down all day long and it was unbearably hot. My eyes stung with the heat and dust, and the blinding light. Everywhere was the colour of sand. Here the greenery and the shade – even the rain – were very soothing. Being in the park was like pain relief for the eyes. And I knew that when we went back home a fantastic meal would be waiting for us.

Yet it can be hard to escape the experience of having fought in the most dangerous place on the planet. On one occasion we had gone out as a family and were in Radnor Park, in the centre of Folkestone. The kids were chasing after each other and laughing, and Sumitra and I were sitting on a wooden bench watching them. It was a lovely summer's day and could not have been more peaceful.

Then there was a loud bang – a car backfiring or tyre bursting. My body thought it was an enemy attack and reacted before my mind had time to engage. I dropped to the prone position, adrenaline pumping. Sumitra and the kids could not believe what they were seeing. I laughed it off. It was the same when I saw unattended packages – my immediate thought was that it was an IED. But slowly my body and mind adjusted and I became much less jumpy.

Just when I was really relaxing and getting used to being at home, I had to start thinking about going back. That was the worst part of being home on leave. Two weeks is no time at all. After the first week you start counting the days you have left. You want to enjoy them, to squeeze every last second out of them. But then they seem to pass too quickly and you get anxious, dreading the moment you have to leave again, to tear yourself away from the people you love most. With two days to go it really hits you. Soon I will not hear the kids calling my name around the house any more. Soon I'll be alone again at night, with no one to use my arms as a pillow …

I would try to reassure Sumitra that where I was going back to really was not that dangerous. But she never believed that, especially after the loss of my close numberi and guruji. The whole Gurkha community was shocked by those tragedies. The families discussed them endlessly and got really anxious for their sons and husbands who were going back to Afghanistan. Sumitra promised she would pray every day for my safe return. And she made me promise I would take extra care.

This was not just for me. It was for our family. If anything happened to me she would be left to bring up the kids on her own. The kids would be deprived of their father. It would be misery and uncertainty for them all. I had similar conversations on the phone with my mum and dad in Nepal. They depended on me too. And they knew that where I was going back to was a hell on earth.

One night left. My army patrol pack is sorted and waiting for me in the spare room. Next to it my water bottle is filled and ready for the journey. Sumitra cooked rice and pork curry for dinner, and we had some of the dried meat that I always took back as a treat for my bhaiharu. Then we relaxed on the sofa in the living room, Alisa and Anish in my arms. This could be the last time I held them.

I never wanted to let them go. But I reminded myself I had a duty to fulfil. A tradition to maintain. A responsibility to my section, my platoon and my company. I was a husband and father but I was also a warrior. Now was my chance to prove that I was a fearless soldier fit to compare with my forefathers, who had fought so valiantly in so many previous campaigns.

In the morning, as we waited for the minibus to pick me up, no one said very much. In fact it was so quiet you could hear the clock ticking on the wall. I felt very emotional. After all, the next time I came home it could be in a wooden box. But I did not want them to see that. I had to be strong.

I looked each of them in the eyes and smiled, and they smiled back. They were trying to be strong too. Sumitra had lit some traditional oil lamps and we prayed to an image of our God. Then we ate yoghurt, another tradition when someone is going on a journey. It means that whatever happens to them they will always come back.

The first time I had to say goodbye to my wife was the worst. I had been in the army three years by then and had returned to my village to marry Sumitra. When the moment came for me to return to the UK we were all very emotional. She was in tears and so were my mother and sister. My father was trying hard not to show his feelings but I could see how upset he was. So I had a lot of practice at these goodbyes, but they were always difficult moments.

Now, with the minibus due any second, Sumitra told me one more time to take extra care of myself. The kids raised their hands to say goodbye. Then Anish tried to run towards me and Sumitra had to hold him back. He was crying, too young to understand why I was going. The minibus had arrived outside.

'I won't be gone long, Anish,' I said. 'And I'll bring you a toy gun. I promise. OK?'

He nodded, looking so miserable it broke my heart.

'Daddy will be back soon,' said Sumitra.

Then we all looked at each other and I was out of the door and into the minibus. One last look through the windows. Anish stepping towards the minibus with his arm outstretched. Sumitra holding on to him. Then the minibus moved off and I switched my gaze to the front.

A few of my bhaiharu were already on board. We stopped to pick up more. The conversation was all about the leave we had had. Some had even been to Nepal and back. We all agreed we had had a fantastic time. I felt the bond between us returning. This too was my family. Eventually, the conversation dried up. It was a long drive to RAF Brize Norton. Some people fell asleep. Others returned to their private thoughts. As I gazed out of the window at the green countryside I kept seeing Anish walking towards me with his arm reaching out. I could not get him out of my head.

For the return journey we flew to an RAF base in the Middle East and picked up the C130 there. The flight to Camp Bastion was always too long – too much time to think about what you had left behind, too much time to think ahead to what you were walking into. I talked a bit to my bhaiharu – we discussed how long there was still to go on the tour and told stupid jokes. But it was so noisy in the back of the Hercules that it was not easy to hold a conversation.

When I got hungry I thought of Sumitra's cooking, but had to make do with a packed lunch of sandwiches and biscuits. I leaned back in the narrow seat and thought of my comfortable bed at home. As we approached Camp Bastion we all went quiet. I felt in my pocket and clutched my lucky coin. The C130 came down steeply and hit the runway hard.

We hit the ground hard too. We were no longer husbands, sons or dads. We were soldiers. Doing our drills, polishing our skills, honing our alertness. We were back in the land of bullets and bombs, where a split-second loss of concentration could mean that the next time we went home it would be in a wooden box.

CHAPTER 14

HOURS OF NEED

In June 2016, a minibus taking security guards to the Canadian Embassy in Kabul, the capital of Afghanistan, was attacked by a Taliban suicide bomber. The majority of the guards were Nepalese, ex-Indian Gurkhas or Nepalese Army. At least twelve were killed – more, according to some reports. I did not know them personally, but losing them was still like losing brothers. I followed the reaction of their families in Nepal on Facebook and shared their grief.

This tragedy made me want to take revenge on the battle-field. But by this stage I was beyond combat duties. In April 2016, 2 RGR was deployed to Kabul as part of Operation Toral, the codename for the security operation in support of NATO's

Resolute Support Mission in Afghanistan. The purpose of this mission was to train and assist Afghan security forces in their ongoing conflict with the Taliban and other extremist organizations.

I was serving as Regimental Quartermaster Sergeant at Kabul International Airport, known as Hamid Karzai International Airport, where we were responsible for all the resources for the UK forces deployed on Operation Toral. It was an administrative and logistical role that, for much of the time, seemed a long way away from the hotspots of Helmand. But Kabul could be deadly too, as that attack on the minibus proved.

From the window of my office I could see the transport planes landing and departing, carrying all the kit and equipment required to resource and replenish a modern army far from home. I had a desk full of papers. Telephones. Maps on the wall. So much to do there was not much time to think. But occasionally the world beyond Kabul would intrude on my thoughts. A moment stands out. The moment when my world began to change forever. It was 1100 hours on 13 November 2016 – the final month of my final tour of Afghanistan.

Suddenly, out of nowhere, I thought of my mother and missed her so much it was like a physical pain. I had the idea that something had happened and she needed me right at that moment. The last time I had seen her was back in the UK, when she and my father had spent five months with me and my family before returning to Nepal.

That had been eight months before, but every moment was still vivid in my memory and my heart. Recently, my sister

Gudiya had mentioned to me that Mum had been ill. She was not eating properly and complained of headaches. She also had a history of heart disease. But Gudiya said it was nothing to worry about. Now I felt I had to speak to Mum urgently.

Using my welfare phone card (which gave me free calls home) I called the number of my parents in Nepal. It was one hour and fifteen minutes later over there. The middle of the day. I heard the ring tone. I imagined the sound of it in the new home I had built for them away from the mountains, in a town called Charali, near the city of Birtamod. Mum answered.

'Hello? Who's this?'

'Aama, *Namaskar*' (meaning 'Hello'), I replied in the traditional, respectful way.

'*Namaskar hi Kancha!*' (which means 'youngest and dearest'). I could hear the nervous excitement in her voice. She was so surprised she did not know what to say for a second or two.

'Gudiya told me you have not been well,' I said. 'So how are you today? Are you feeling better, Aama?'

'Yes, Kailash, I'm fine. I was feeling a bit poorly for two or three days but I'm better now. God is with us. Please do not worry about me. How are *you*? Remind me, how long do you have left of the tour? I pray for you each day. Please take care of yourself over there, Kancha.'

'I'm fine,' I said. 'Glad to hear you are too. Tell me about Gudiya.' My sister was married and due to have her first baby any minute.

'Gudiya is very well,' she said and told me all about my sister's pregnancy. On the surface Mum sounded normal but

215

I could tell she was worried about something. She finished by saying that my current tour of Afghanistan seemed to be taking forever. 'Take extra care of yourself,' she said. By this point we were both in tears.

The next day I got a message from my sister on Facebook that Mum was getting worse by the hour. Gudiya and my father had decided to drive her to hospital in Birtamod, about 10 km away, near the border with India, and she would let me know how things were.

The following day my sister called to say my mother had been admitted to the Intensive Care Unit (ICU) and that she was in good hands. However, she showed no improvement. I decided to apply for compassionate leave and received permission to leave for Nepal on 17 November. The night before, I could not sleep. I felt much more fear than on the eve of a dangerous battle – fear at the state I would find my mother in when I reached the hospital. Also impatience. I just wanted to get there.

An alarm clock was by my bed, ready to wake me for an early start. I kept looking at the luminous hands in the dark. They barely seemed to move. When I closed my eyes, trying to sleep, I travelled back to my childhood. Saw my mother laughing at things I had done. Even crying when I brought her damp firewood. But always loving. I would smile to myself in my half-sleep – but then I would open my eyes and see the shapes of my kit on the table, packed and ready for the journey. I prayed that she would be OK. It was one of the longest nights I have spent.

0700 hours on 17 November. I was waiting in the line at passport control at Hamid Karzai International Airport with a British Army Officer, who spoke Pashto, and a Gurkha colleague. I was dressed in civvies, but wearing army boots with my army patrol pack on my back. The other people in the queue were all Afghanis. Maybe I was imagining it but I felt they were all looking at me suspiciously, wondering what I was doing and where I was going. I stayed cool on the outside but inside I was pumped up, ready for anything.

It took ages to reach the front of the line. But eventually it was my turn and I handed over my documents (Nepalese passport and British Army ID card). The immigration officer was like immigration officers the world over – stern and suspicious. They must all go to the same training school. This one spent a few seconds flicking through the pages of my passport, past the stamps for UK, Brunei, Malaysia and Singapore. Then he threw it down on the counter and looked up at me with weary eyes.

'No visa,' he said.

No visa? This did not make sense. It was true that my Nepalese passport did not have a visa allowing entry to Afghanistan, but I did not need one because I had a military ID card which certified me as a member of ISAF (the International Security Assistance Force). The immigration officer seemed to be saying that I needed an entry visa in my passport before I could leave. My army colleague who spoke Pashto tried to intervene. He explained that I was a British soldier and I was travelling to Nepal on compassionate leave. My documents were in order. What was the problem?

'No visa, no visa!' Now the immigration officer was shouting. We refused to budge. Eventually, he summoned the airport manager. We went over the same ground with him. He too got angry and started shouting. I remained calm and respectful. But inside I was boiling. If he wanted to play the angry game he had picked the wrong man.

It was important not to react aggressively. The last thing I wanted was to attract attention. The airport was heavily guarded and supposed to be a secure zone. But this was Afghanistan. In separate incidents in the previous two years a suicide bomber and a gunman had killed several people just outside the airport. Nowhere was safe.

One of my fears, as we stood arguing about my passport, was being kidnapped. Already I was checking out the layout of the terminal building, working out an escape plan in case we were approached by the wrong kind of people. It was simple: I would run. Run out of the building and all the way back to the military base, which was less than 2 km away.

But what if they chased me in a vehicle? Bundled me in and drove off to a dark dungeon? We had all heard the stories of the cruel punishments and deaths inflicted on captured military personnel. My mind was racing. I felt claustrophobic. All I wanted to do was get out of that terminal building and on to a plane that would take me far away from this crazy world, and into the arms of my suffering and beloved mother.

By now I was letting my Pashto-speaking colleague do all the talking. I avoided eye contact, appeared calm, kept checking out the immediate surroundings for suspicious-looking characters. And finally the issue was resolved as quickly as it had begun. What changed? I have no idea. But suddenly the immigration officer was handing me back my passport and waving me through, and I was shaking hands with my two colleagues, who wished me a safe journey.

Sitting in the waiting room, waiting to board the flight to Delhi, I felt every eye upon me. I was practically the only foreigner there. And my boots and patrol pack made it obvious I was a soldier. I looked straight ahead, avoiding eye contact and praying that the forty minutes to departure would pass as quickly as possible.

The reason I was so nervous, I realized, was that this was the first time in the whole of my many months and tours in Afghanistan that I had been without a weapon. To feel like a sitting target in the most dangerous and violent country on earth, and know that your only defence are your fists and your wits is very unsettling.

Finally, they called the flight but my worries were not over. From the departure gate to the plane we had to take a bus. This triggered an immediate alarm in my head. A favourite target of suicide bombers was crowded, soft-skinned vehicles like this. As the bus rolled slowly across the tarmac towards the steps of the plane I watched my fellow passengers anxiously. When the doors opened and everyone rushed to get off I felt a surge of relief.

The rest of the journey passed uneventfully. In Delhi I changed planes for the Nepalese capital, Kathmandu, arriving there at midnight. Early the next morning I took a short flight to Bhadrapur Airport near Birtamod, and then it was a short taxi ride to Charali where my parents and sister were now living. When I got there my father was asleep in the sitting room. He had moved there at night so he could be near the telephone in case anyone called from the hospital.

It was an emotional reunion. I kneeled down and touched his feet with my forehead and he placed the palm of his hand on the top of my head – the traditional blessing between father and son. We talked about my journey. All the time I was thinking how much he had aged in the few months since I had last seen him, back in the UK. He had grown a long, straggly beard and looked weak and thin. The stress he was going through over my mother's health was taking its toll.

Dad told me Gudiya had given birth to a daughter the day before by Caesarean section, in another hospital in Birtamod. Now I was even more impatient to get on the road. I dumped my bags, splashed my face with water and was back out of the door, promising to stay in touch.

The taxi ride to the hospital was a short one. At the reception desk I was directed to the ICU. I introduced myself to the staff and was told to wait. Now I was so nervous I practically needed to be admitted myself. My heart was racing. How poorly would she be?

After what seemed an endless wait a nurse said I could go in to my mother's room. She was in a bed in the far corner, hooked up to medical equipment. We locked eyes. So many times on the phone she had told me not to come to see her: it was too much trouble; the journey was difficult; there was really no need, she was fine. But now I knew, by the look in her eyes, I had done the right thing.

These were her hours of need. I was shocked by her appearance. She was being given oxygen through a face mask. She had lost weight and looked gaunt. There was no doubt she was gravely ill. I sat next to the bed and held her hand, trying desperately not to let my shock and concern show in my face. But I could not stop my tears flowing.

My mother was stronger than me. She put on a brave face. 'So, Kailash, you're here!' she said. 'You came all this way by plane?'

'By plane, yes.' I nodded, blinking away the tears.

Then she looked me in the eye. A look of tenderness and fear that said so much. I had no words to say to her, just my love to give. After a while she tried to be cheerful again. 'So your sister had a baby girl yesterday,' she said.

'Dad told me. I'm going to see her later.'

'She'll be so happy to see you, Kancha!'

I squeezed her hand. After a few more minutes the nurse came in and signalled that I should leave so she could get some rest. I took this opportunity to go and see my sister in the hospital nearby. On the way I was thinking how uncertain my life suddenly seemed. The thing about the army is that it runs on a strict and constant routine. Now I felt that order being taken away from me. I hardly knew where I was or what I should do next.

Our family, which had seemed so strong and unbreakable, now seemed very fragile with Mum so ill, Dad getting old and frail and my sister at a new stage in her life. Gudiya was as devoted to Mum as I was. But she had a new life to consider, and this would take up all her time as our mother neared the end of hers.

It was nearly four years since I had last seen my sister. When I reached her room a friend of hers was there. Her friend smiled at me and held her finger to her lips. Gudiya was sleeping. Her beautiful baby was in her arms. When I saw them all my worry melted away. This was my kid sister, eleven years younger than me. She had been just six years old when I left the village to become a soldier. Now here she was, a first-time mother.

I watched her for a few minutes then called her name softly. 'Gudiya, Gudiya. It's me, *dai*' (meaning 'older brother').

She did not wake up so I tried again. Then her friend gently shook her shoulder. Gudiya opened her eyes, stared at me and let out a cry of joy.

These were a lovely few minutes, when we admired the new baby and joked about the past. But soon the conversation turned to our mother's health. And at this point Gudiya stopped talking and could not look at me. She buried her face in the blanket and started to cry.

I held her hand tight and told her not to worry. Her husband could not be with her because he was working abroad, but I said she was not alone and I would take care of everything. By now the room was filling up with her husband's family. I chatted with them for a few minutes then said I was going back to see Mum.

My tiredness and all the competing emotions got the better of me as I left the hospital. I just burst into tears. Then a strange thing happened. I was so tired that instead of walking back to the hospital where Mum was I decided to get an auto-rickshaw, a little three-wheeler taxi. It was early evening and the traffic congestion, which is always bad, was at its worst.

As my driver wove in and out between the cars I was not paying any attention to what was happening on the street. Then a horn blasted in my ear and I looked up to see a forty-seater bus heading for our rickshaw at high speed. The bus driver had lost control. My driver swerved, the bus missed us by a whisker and crashed into a metal pole at the side of the road.

Those flimsy rickshaws are just glorified mopeds. They offer no protection in a collision. There is no doubt that if the bus had hit us the driver and I would have been killed. This was another extraordinary twist in a traumatic day. The crash was a bad one and the rickshaw driver wanted to stop and help. But I could not take any more misery or complication. I just wanted to see my mum again.

As I walked into the hospital the first victims of the bus crash were being taken into the emergency room, screaming and crying. But I went straight to the ICU where the doctor in charge of my mother's treatment discussed her case with me. He confirmed that she was gravely ill. Her heart was not working properly, she had liver damage and was suffering from jaundice. He said he was going to prescribe a new drug, which should certainly relieve her pain. When I asked if she could make a full recovery he said it was possible. This cheered me up for a moment, until I realized he was probably just telling me what I wanted to hear.

I was not allowed in to see my mum that night. I stood at the door of her room watching her through the little window. She was tossing and turning and looked restless. I longed to go inside and comfort her. But at least I was allowed to stay overnight in the ICU so I could be near her.

I had brought a sleeping bag, which I unrolled in a corridor, next to other relatives of ICU patients. I lay down and shut my eyes. It was difficult for me to deal with this. Many times on the battlefield I had faced danger and death, but I had always known what to do. I had always found a way of fighting back. I had never given up hope. Now, as I lay staring at the ceiling of the corridor, it was hard for me to find much hope in my mother's situation.

It was impossible to get much sleep. The mosquitoes were driving me crazy and there were frequent emergencies when the staff spoke urgently and there was the sound of running feet. Each time I wondered if it was my mother, if she had stopped breathing. Sometimes a nurse would appear and ask the relative of a patient to go to the pharmacy on the ground floor to buy more medicine. I was expecting it to happen to me, which kept me tense and awake all night. But I was never asked.

The sun rose on a new day and after I had washed and had something to eat I felt more optimistic. I remembered the doctor's words and had faith in the new drugs. At 1000 hours I was allowed in to see my mother. I entered the room expecting to see a real improvement, a smile on her face, even. What I saw shocked and angered me.

She still had the oxygen mask on and a drip was feeding medication into a cannula on her arm. Then I noticed, as she turned her head slowly towards me, that her hands were tied to the side of the bed with white nylon cord. My immediate thought was that she was being treated like a criminal or an animal. I turned to the nurse, who was following me into the room. 'What the hell's going on?'

'I'm sorry, sir,' she said. 'It's for her own good. Your mother kept trying to pull her oxygen mask off and pull the drip out of her arm.'

I wanted to cry when I heard this, but knew I had to be strong. 'How are you, Mum? Feeling better? You're looking good!'

She stared around the room, as if wondering where she was, then said, 'A little better, thank you, Kancha.'

I did not know what to say next and, as I hesitated, she started talking in a flood of words, not always making sense: 'I don't know, Kancha. How's life going to be? I can't move. I can't move my body. I'm really sorry but I can't help you. I can't help anybody. How's Gudiya? Did you see Gudiya? How's her baby? Is it a boy or a girl? Tell her I can't help her. She probably thinks I'm a terrible mother!'

I grasped her hand tight. 'Aama. Don't worry. I'm looking after Gudiya. She and the baby are fine. She'll be back home soon and then Dad will look after her, too. The baby's a beautiful girl, by the way. A real princess.'

According to tradition Mum had the honour of naming Gudiya's baby daughter. I reminded her of this and after a moment she said, 'Gudiya's daughter's name will be Kanchi Maya, OK?'

I nodded. 'OK. Maya is a lovely name. Thank you.'

'Look, Kailash,' my mother continued. 'There are four beautiful babies right here and they don't cry. See? They haven't eaten since yesterday and still they don't cry. Oh look. Mangdahane Maeela is outside with some other people. Better invite them in. Make sure you offer them some tea. It's getting late Kancha. We need to go.'

There were no babies, of course. Not in the entire hospital, never mind in the same room as us. The only people outside were other patients and their relatives. My mum's mind had wandered back to Khebang, the village where I grew up. She was getting worse. She could hardly keep her eyes open for more than a few minutes at a time. Her hands were trembling badly.

There was only one thing to do. If she were to have any chance at all of recovery I had to get her to a better hospital. This was Nepal, a poor country compared to its neighbour, India. The doctors and nurses tried their best, but medical facilities and treatment here were quite basic. I decided I would take my mum across the border and pay for her treatment at the hospital in the Indian city of Silguri, a distance of less than 50 km. It was a relief to be able to take some positive action, rather than just sit there helplessly and watch her fade away.

First of all I called the hospital in Silguri to inform them of my mother's case and check they could take her. This was arranged. A bed would be waiting. Then I informed the doctor currently looking after her of my plan and asked him to discharge her immediately. He agreed that she would receive better treatment and medications in India, and completed the necessary paperwork.

I called my father at home and told him what was happening. I did not want to let on how bad Mum was – I just said that she deserved the best and I was determined to do all I could. Finally, I nipped to the hospital down the road to inform Gudiya and see my newborn niece, who now had a name. Gudiya was doing fine and due to be discharged that day. She and the baby were going to return to the village where Dad would look after them.

An ambulance was waiting at Mum's hospital, and some relatives who lived in Birtamod had turned up to help with the transfer. It was a real morale-booster to see them and know I was not doing this alone. The first thing we had to do was get her from the ICU to the ambulance. There were no lifts in the hospital. We had to carry her down by stretcher.

As we were bringing her down she looked up at me and said, 'I can't carry any firewood, you know. And where's my khukuri? You need to get it ready for me.'

'Don't worry, Mum. I'll take care of everything. Just you relax.'

'Where are we going?'

'To somewhere where you'll get better.'

During the journey in the ambulance she winced in pain every time we drove over bumps in the road. For the whole way the lights were flashing and the siren was blaring. Some cars pulled over to let us pass but the journey still seemed to take forever. When she started drifting off I shook her gently, worried that if she fell asleep she might not wake up. After two hours we made it to the hospital. The medical team were on hand to whisk her straight to the ICU.

A feeling of relief flooded over me. It was as if I had been holding my breath the entire journey, and finally I could breathe properly. I had done all I could for her. She was in the best possible hands. What happened next was down to fate. I thought of time flowing. How quickly it passes sometimes, like water when the river is high. Impossible to stop. I feared Mum's time was coming.

Once she had been taken up to the ICU most of the family members who had accompanied me to Silguri went back to Birtamod. Just one of my cousins stayed with me for company. We booked a room in a hotel just a few minutes' walk from the hospital. Then we returned to the hospital where the doctor said it was better to let her rest and to come back in the morning. I left my mobile phone number in case anything happened in the night.

In the hotel room my cousin quickly got his head down but I could not sleep. I worried that Mum would wake up and wonder where she was. She had never been on her own in another country before. She spoke only Nepali and could not understand Hindi all that well. Maybe she would think I had abandoned her. Every few minutes I checked my phone in case there was a message from the hospital. Eventually I could not stand it any more. I got up as quietly as I could, put on some clothes, and crept out of the hotel and along to the hospital. It was still dark and must have been about 0300 hours.

At the reception desk I explained who I was, and asked the duty clerk to call the ICU for an update on my mother. She spoke on the phone, looked up at me and smiled. 'She's sleeping well. Nothing to worry about. You need to get some sleep yourself. You're not helping her by fretting.'

She was right. I returned to the hotel with a weight lifted off my shoulders and slept like a baby for the rest of the night. At 1000 hours the next morning I went back to the hospital with a renewed sense of hope. This was India. They had outstanding doctors and facilities here. They might just be able to turn things around.

Outside the doors to the ICU a queue of relatives was already waiting. A security guard was letting people in on a one-in-one-out basis. When it was my turn I rushed in to find her fast asleep. I sat by the bed and held her hand. 'Aama!' I said softly. 'Aama, Aama!' She did not wake. She was attached to a heart monitor that beeped regularly to her heartbeat. I waited a few more seconds then spoke her name softly again. Tears were rolling down her cheeks. I wiped them away with a tissue. Those tears broke my heart. Was she in physical pain? Was she frightened?

She opened her eyes and focused on my face. 'Oh, Kailash,' she said. 'Where have you been? I've been waiting for ever and ever. How is Gudiya? Has she gone back home yet? What about you? You must be starving. Go and get something to

229

eat. I know you've spent a fortune on my treatment but I'm fine now. We need to go.'

I fought back the tears as I replied, 'Aama, listen. Gudiya has been discharged from hospital, and she and the baby are back at home. Dad will be making them chicken soup. Remember his delicious chicken soup? And don't worry about the money.'

When she fell asleep again I placed her hand on the bedclothes and left the room to speak to her doctor. 'She's stabilized,' he said. 'We just have to hope the medication starts to work. We need to give it time.'

Relatives of ICU patients could visit them twice a day, at 1000 hours and 1800 hours. I built my routine around those times. On the second day my cousin returned to his family, leaving me feeling even more alone. I spent hours on end in the hotel room, staring at the ceiling. I cried. I prayed to God. These were some of the longest days of my life.

On my visits to the hospital I brought Mum some simple snacks and fruit juice. She tried her best to eat and drink, but over the days there was no improvement in her health. In fact she seemed to be getting worse. She was sleeping more and more. Sometimes she sweated profusely. I felt useless. All I could do was hold her hand, mop her brow and blow cool air over her when she was over-heating.

At one point she said, 'Kancha, we have to go home now. Have you seen the time? It's getting late. But I won't be able to walk very easily. Can you make me a stick? My father keeps calling me.'

Her father, my grandfather, had died four years before.

She was talking to the dead. It was as if she was already half-way to the next world.

As the days passed I had to face the fact that she was not going to get better. She was on her final journey. And for that she needed her family with her. I called my wife in the UK and we made arrangements for her to come over with our children. It was a long journey for Sumitra and the kids. When they got to the hospital they hardly knew what day it was. It gave me such a lift to see them, though. They waited anxiously outside Mum's room till I ushered them in. 'Look who's here to see you, Aama. They've come halfway round the world just for you!'

My mum smiled the biggest smile when she saw who it was. But she could not speak any words by then. When my wife took her hand and said, 'How are you, Aama, are you OK?', she just nodded, and smiled, and closed her eyes.

Other family members – including Mum's two brothers, my uncles – who lived locally also arrived to give their support. It went on like this for a few days. Then, on the afternoon of 3 December 2016, the doctor in charge of her treatment asked to speak to me.

'I think she's ready to go home,' he said. I did not understand what he meant at first. He had to spell it out. 'She's not getting any better. She could go at any time. Better if she's at home when it happens.'

This news put me in a state of shock. Although rationally I had known she was dying, I had clung to the hope that treatment in India would somehow cure her. I asked for some time to think it over. After I left the hospital I felt dizzy and sick. I sat on a bench with my family and relatives standing around me and I cried like a baby.

We needed to make the transport arrangements and get her ready as soon as possible. For me it was an admission of failure. I felt crushed. I called my sister, who was now back at the family home so she could get everything ready. Then the nurses packed up her belongings and helped her into fresh clothes for the journey. All the time she lay there limp, her eyes opening and closing, barely registering her surroundings.

'We're going home today,' I said. 'We'll be seeing Dad again, and Gudiya, and Gudiya's new baby. Kanchi Maya. Remember?' My wife repeated what I had said. 'Home, Aama. We're going home.' But she did not react.

I told myself that once we got home the familiar surroundings would give her a lift. Our family would be together again, for the first time in a long while. We could really enjoy the days she had left. She would die happy and secure.

As we prepared to leave, the nurses put Mum on a ventilator to give her a boost of oxygen. I rushed off to the hospital pharmacy to buy the medication and other supplies she had been prescribed. Hospital orderlies brought her down on a stretcher and transferred her to the ambulance. I climbed in with her two younger brothers while my wife, kids and the rest of the family followed in two rented cars.

The journey began. The traffic back to the border, and west towards Birtamod, was heavy. The ambulance drivers kept the lights and sirens on. I took Mum's hand and whispered in her ear. 'Aama, Aama.'

She was asleep. I shook her shoulder gently. She stirred and struggled for breath as if she was trying to speak. Then she went back to sleep. I waggled her toes. I called again. 'Wake up!' No reaction. I left it for a few minutes, telling myself she was just in a deep sleep. I tried again. She did not react. Then I felt the heat in the ambulance. I began to sweat. My heart speeded up and my breath came in short bursts. I could hardly breathe. My whole body was shaking. I felt like I was having a heart attack. 'Aama, Aama, Aama.'

I stopped shaking her. Her mouth and eyes were closed. Her ears were no longer hearing. Her face looked peaceful. I touched her arm, her face. Felt the warmth of her. My uncles tried to comfort me. One said, 'It comes to us all, Kailash. One day we have to leave this earth. This is her time.' But I would not be comforted. I called out again. I could not stop crying. I hoped that somewhere deep in her heart she still heard me.

I had dreaded this moment and now it was here I could not believe it. Images came into my mind. Our home, our road, the banana trees she planted in Khebang, her vegetables in the garden at Charali, her bedroom, her bamboo baskets, her flip-flops. Recently, when I spoke to her on the phone from Afghanistan, she had referred to her coming death. 'The sun is slipping behind the mountain,' she said. 'Soon it will set forever.'

'Not for a long time yet.' I replied. But now it had happened.

That terrible ambulance journey continued with my head full of thoughts and emotions. I cried. I called out her name. Soon I would never speak the word 'Aama' again. I could not keep my eyes from her face. Soon I would never see it again.

All the time I held her hand, and sometimes I touched her arm or her feet.

Finally, in the early evening, we reached the family home at Charali. The scenes that followed were too heart rending to go through. For my sister this should have been one of the happiest times of her life. Her daughter, Kanchi Maya, was only two weeks old. She was so proud of her, and had been looking forward so much to Mum seeing her and holding her granddaughter in her arms.

Instead Gudiya was so overcome with grief that she almost fainted. My father was in a state of shock and stood there in a daze. For me it was time to be strong. Inside I was in pieces, but I put on a brave front as we brought Mum into the house and placed her in the front room.

We stayed up the whole night, watching her, being with her, saying prayers. The night passed surprisingly quickly and in the early morning I felt calm. I knew what I had to do, the final task I would perform for her. My sister, my wife and other female relatives dressed Mum in her newest and finest clothes – a sari we bought for her in Brunei, shoes from the UK.

Then other family members arrived at the house. They prepared a bamboo stretcher. We placed her body on it and covered her with a white cloth in the traditional manner. Meanwhile people from the local village had gathered outside the house. They expressed their appreciation to the family, telling us that Mum was the kindest person they knew. That meant so much.

At 1130 hours my uncle and nephews and I hoisted the stretcher on to our shoulders and carried Mum the 200 m to a waiting hearse. I travelled in the hearse with my wife, my dad and my sister, with other family members and friends following in their own cars. The burial plot was in a forest not far away.

There we lifted her body and, as is the custom, circled the grave clockwise three times with her to symbolize her final journey before placing her in a wooden coffin. I touched her feet with my forehead and we said a blessing. Then we lowered the coffin into the deep grave. It was a terrible moment, to know I would never see her again. We were all crying. We were saying goodbye to a precious part of ourselves. We would never be the same again.

The final act of the burial was to place bricks on the top of the coffin and fill in the rest of the hole with earth. Afterwards we stood in silence looking at the patch of freshly dug earth. There was nothing more to be done here. We returned home where the local dhami said prayers to ensure Mum would rest in peace in heaven for eternity.

Mum had gone but she was everywhere in that house. Her clothes and possessions were still here. And when I saw the fruit and vegetables she had planted in the garden I broke down. I heard her voice: 'Now you're a soldier you need to make sure you eat properly and get enough rest, Kailash. You hear me?' I was waiting for her to walk through the front door. Or when I entered a room, for her to be there. At meal times there was a gap where she used to sit that I could not help looking at. When we watched TV I waited for her to make funny comments.

In the days following her death I tried to be more positive. What had happened was just part of the natural cycle of life and death. Although my mother was no longer here physically, she lived on in my heart and mind. Everything I had done was down to her. She was my inspiration.

This brief period at the family home after the funeral was like a bridge between my past and the future I would have to face without her. Soon the time came to leave and go back out into the world. As I lay in bed on the final morning I wrote my mum a letter in my head. And I realized, while I was writing it, it was not just addressed to my mother. It was to all those I had loved and lost and who will be with me forever. The letter went something like this:

> *Dearest Aama. I want you to know, in your little corner of heaven, that you do not need to worry about us down here. None of us. I will look after the family, and I know that you will look after me. And now that you are at peace I want you to enjoy yourself! Eat well, sleep well, be happy, as you used to say to me. And don't, whatever you do, work too hard. You did enough of that down here!*
>
> *Wherever I am, and whatever I am doing, I will think of you. And, if you don't mind, I will sometimes ask you for your guidance. Life, as we know, is a difficult journey and some of the steps along the way can be very tough. In the past you have helped me get over difficult times with your love, your kindness*

and wisdom. I will never forget those moments. And for sure there will be more in the future. So don't be surprised when I come to you again with the question, 'Aama, what should I do?'

Meanwhile, please prepare me a nice home where you are. Get the food ready! The tea and coffee. And don't forget plenty of water. We have to stay hydrated at all times! Please be patient and wait for me. Be ready to take me in your arms again. Because one day I will be taking the same route as you. The same route as all of us. It is just a matter of time.

Your dearest son, Kailash.

CHAPTER 15

CLEAR AND SEARCH

The images of the brave brothers I had lost, Yubraj and Krishna, stayed with me for the rest of my time in Afghanistan. Krishna travelling in the Warrior infantry fighting vehicle that was hit by an IED. The infectious smile of my dearest numberi, Yubraj, as he hugged me and shook my hand for the last time at Camp Bastion. The memory of his coffin being loaded on to the C130 and the plane's rear doors closing. At odd moments these images would come to me.

It happened often in the heat of battle. I remember being pinned down by the Taliban while the platoon was on a clear-and-search operation about 16 km south of Garmsir. The section I was commanding came under IDF attack, and we had to dive for cover under our Jackal.

It was 1100 hours local time. My goggles got broken. My eyes, nose and mouth were full of dust. Our bodies were under the vehicle but our legs were poking out. If the Jackal was hit we would be finished. None of us spoke. We all understood the gravity of the situation. The shells were exploding around us. My knees and elbows were hurting like hell from when I hit the ground. I screwed my eyes shut and waited for it to stop.

But the attack seemed to go on for ever. Every second that passed I feared would be my last. That was when I thought of my brothers, Yubraj and Krishna guruji, and wondered if I was about to join them. And then I did what I always did in these life-or-death situations. I reached into my pocket and held my lucky coin as tightly as I could.

There was really nothing we could do but wait it out. It was impossible to return fire as these projectiles were probably being launched from miles away. The barrage paused for a few seconds – then started up again. We stayed where we were. Another pause, then more shells coming in. Eventually, though, the rounds stopped for long enough for us to decide to move.

The Platoon Commander, Lt Crawley, instructed us to continue on our present axis of advance. Our group of eight Jackal and Viking vehicles drove down into a steep-sided valley and through a small river. We dismounted, checking around the river crossing for enemy IEDs. Ahead of us was our Area of Responsibility, a patchwork of buildings, open fields, irrigation ditches and tree-lines where we knew the enemy had been operating.

The Jackals and Vikings were parked up on slightly higher ground so they could provide covering fire as we progressed. We set out in single file with my point man, Dipendra, leading and me directly behind him. The rest of the platoon was coming up in tactical formation behind us – forming up to present as small a target as possible. This was the first time we had been active in the area. We did not know the terrain and were unfamiliar with how the local Taliban might react. Initially, the tactical advantage lay with the insurgents. They were hiding and watching our advance. They knew the locality, had all the routes covered and could launch an ambush at any time. It was really hot and we were sweating heavily, having to rub the sweat from our eyes. We were pumped up, eyes darting everywhere. Then Dipendra was whispering back to me, 'Fighting-age male running to corner of that building, guruji.' He pointed. 'Can I fire a warning shot, guruji?'

I told him not to fire. I wanted to see if any more insurgents would appear. The man Dipendra had spotted could be a look-out who was passing back information to a bigger fighting group. We were approaching a small house. I ran forward to the corner of the house and took up a kneeling position. Before scanning the buildings and ground ahead I tried to steady my breathing, which came in rapid gasps.

If I could locate the enemy I could work out a plan of action, always applying our ROE. Moving from building to building like this, close to a dense urban area, was highly dangerous. One well-aimed bullet from an unseen fighter could put you down forever. Combating this threat required vigilance, leadership, decisive action. Yes, they had the advantage, but we were the professionals. We were trained to find them and hunt them down, and that's what we were going to do.

Dipendra and the rest of my section joined me at the corner of the house. They leant on the wall behind my shoulder waiting for me to give the next order. 'Hold there, bhaiharu,' I said. I crawled forward beyond the cover of the building to get a better view of the buildings 30-50 m ahead. I pressed my PRR transmitter and spoke in a whisper: 'OK, bhaiharu. There are a number of holes in the buildings on the northern side of our axis of advance. Possible firing points. I want you to cover every hole as we cross. And engage if we contact. Acknowledge 2IC. Over.'

'Roger, out, guruji,' replied 2IC.

As part of the SOP the section was divided into Fire Teams Charlie and Delta. Team Charlie (me and three bhaiharu) would advance while Delta (the other four men) provided the cover. We checked our ammo pouches, weapons and personal kit. All the time I was studying those holes in the walls of the buildings ahead, looking for the glint of gun barrels.

'Fire Team Charlie, prepare to move,' I said on the PRR. Then a few seconds later, 'Move now, move now!'

We ran forward in a zigzag pattern, making us hard to hit. Luckily, less than 15 m ahead was a ditch that was full of water – maybe an irrigation channel for growing corn. It was a good place to take cover as IEDs were not usually waterproof and unlikely to be deployed in water, so we knew it was probably safe. 'Prepare to drop down,' I said. 'Down.'

We dropped into the ditch and took up firing positions with water sloshing about our ankles. We covered the forward ground, scanning buildings ahead and to the south for possible enemy firing points. About 150 m in front were tall stands of bamboo surrounded by poppy fields. These fields of pink and white flowers always looked so beautiful but they were deadly – they produced the opium that fed the drugs trade in the West, and put money in the pockets of insurgents and local warlords.

After a couple of minutes Team Delta joined us in the ditch and we made a base-line – one extended line so that everyone could engage the enemy if needed. By now the water was seeping up my clothing so that half my body was wet. Suddenly, I noticed friendly forces approaching between two small buildings about 350 m to the north. They were entering a field of wheat about knee-high, which provided a certain amount of cover but absolutely no protection.

I informed my bhaiharu – it is vital in the battlefield to be aware at all times of the location of friendly C/S so as to avoid so-called 'blue on blue' fire, being fired at by your own forces in the confusion of battle. It happens unfortunately, especially at night.

As I continued to scan the buildings directly ahead with my naked eye I picked up suspicious movement. Then a man ran fast across my field of vision. He carried a gun and disappeared behind the back of a building about 90 m from our position. I suspected the Taliban were withdrawing to make a base-line of their own.

'Enemy, enemy,' I said, speaking as quietly as I could. I decided to move forward and engage. There was no way of knowing their strength. And they may have been preparing to surprise us by attacking from the southerly side as we advanced. But this was war. Always a risk. My team started to move forward from the ditch, conducting a silent 'fire and movement'.

This is the standard infantry tactic, with one section moving rapidly forward using all available cover, while support forces watch their backs and open fire if the enemy attacks. On this occasion we moved forward a few paces but the enemy did not engage. As we did so I noticed a number of women, children and elderly people moving south from one of the buildings.

The women wore burkas, covering their faces, and could well have been male insurgents in disguise. This was a frequent Taliban practice. So was using civilians as human shields – they knew we were bound by strict ROEs, which meant we could not risk harming civilians in our engagements with the enemy.

We dropped into a prone position and waited until Lt Crawley and the rest of the section were in tactical position behind us, and ready to support as necessary. 'Fire Team Charlie, prepare to move,' I ordered. Pause. Then, 'Move now!'

This time we heard gunfire. The battlefield sound that makes your pulse race and your heart pound.

'Contact front, contact front!' I shouted.

We dropped to the ground, trying to flatten ourselves. There was a barrage of enemy fire. We could be walking into a trap. The enemy could have been waiting for days for us to show up. It certainly felt like that – fire was coming from what seemed like every direction in a series of coordinated attacks. It reminded me of something – the way corn pops when you heat it in a big pot. Pop pop pop all around us.

The incoming rounds were missing their target for now. Flying overhead, hitting the sand and rock around us. But we were sitting ducks. We needed to move. Easier said than done. The intensity of the attack made it difficult to even raise our heads in case we took a bullet. We were being hammered. I had to act. I lifted my head, crawled forward into a firing position and got off a couple of rounds. 'Enemy, enemy!' I yelled.

The rest of the section opened fire. I could now see that most of the trouble was coming from two insurgents embedded at the corner of a building at the far end of the line of bamboos, about 150 m away. I took aim and put down some rounds. Though my chest was heaving I was pretty sure I was accurate. But somehow I missed them. The shots were picking up dirt at the corner of the building.

The fighters vanished from my rifle sight. Maybe I had hit them after all. Then two new fighters appeared at the corner of the same building and fired a few rounds. At the same time shots were coming in from the line of bamboos.

'OK, listen up, bhairharu,' I yelled. 'Enemy on the bamboo tree-line. And from the corner of the building on the left. Seen?'

'Seen, guruji!' they all replied at the same time.

'Rapid fire, rapid fire!' I instructed.

We rained a barrage of bullets on the building and the bamboos. Both targets disappeared in clouds of dust but kept firing back. The noise was deafening. At moments like this you feel conflict is as a battle of wills as well as bullets. But however hard they fought back, we knew we were the better fighters. We'd win.

Gurkhas are patient people, slow to anger. We will not start a fight, but when the battle begins we will see it through to the end. We will never give up, even to the point of sacrificing our own lives. Now, I knew, my bhaiharu ached to get on top of the enemy so they could draw their khukuris. Then they would discover who was braver and stronger.

As the commander of my section I had to be careful at such moments not to let my men follow their instincts and risk their lives. Still, I had to make a difficult decision. Our ammunition was getting low. We could not continue for much longer in this firefight. I decided to launch an attack so we could take them on at close quarters.

'Fire Team Charlie, prepare to move,' I yelled. 'Check mags, check pouches. Move!'

We ran in zigzag fashion for about 8 m.

'Prepare to get down. Down!'

We dropped into firing positions and suppressed the enemy while Team Delta under the command of 2IC followed the same routine and joined us. We moved forward in two more bounds that took us about 100 m from enemy lines. All the time we were suppressing them with heavy fire. Then I realized that friendly fire was coming in from 200 m to the north of our position.

As the bullets flew there was a loud scream and one of our men fell on the north side, where friendly forces were also advancing. Under huge enemy fire he tried to crawl to safety. It was impossible to tell where he had been hit, but I could see the pain and fear on his face as he scrambled in the dust.

We moved forward at speed to reach him before he took another hit, and to support our forces to the north. Between us and them were a group of buildings. We reached them, checked they were clear of enemy fighters and continued the advance, all the while firing away at the enemy.

Two colleagues reached the fallen soldier and pulled him out of the line of fire. It was a lucky escape for him and the men who saved him – extracting casualties on the battlefield can be a highly dangerous operation, as the brave brothers who retrieved my numberi Yubraj at Musa Qala can testify.

The firefight continued as we cleared more buildings. I could no longer see the two insurgents who had been firing at us. But a building directly in front of our current position now aroused my suspicion. There! They were firing through holes to the left and right of the door. I took cover behind a wall no more than 20 m from the suspicious building and adopted a kneeling position. The rest of Team Charlie piled in behind me and awaited my orders.

We were exhausted. It was hot as hell – like ten suns in the sky. Sweat was sloshing off our bodies. Our chests were heaving with exertion. I kept my eyes glued to those holes next to the door. I knew the enemy had the advantage. This was a life or death situation. If they fired on us from such close range we would not stand a chance. And our bullets would be ineffective because they could not penetrate the thick mud walls of the house.

On the other hand, Team Delta were ready about 20 m south of our position to provide fire support. I decided to take the house. '2IC, ready?' I said on the PRR.

'Ready, guruji.' They fired off a couple of rounds.

I turned round and looked into the eyes of my bhaiharu in Team Charlie. 'We're going to clear that building. There's a high chance the enemy are in there. OK?' They nodded. I circled my left index finger in the air, a 'rounding up' motion that meant 'Get ready to move'. The index finger of my right hand was stuck firmly on the trigger of my rifle. Two seconds. Then we went, running zigzag with our guns trained on those firing holes. No bullets came. A couple of seconds and we reached the building. Dipendra and I took up firing positions either side of the door. Our two bhaiharu took the left and right corners of the building as flank protection.

I was really pumped up. Nervous at what might come next. Angry. Now that I was within spitting distance of the enemy, bloody angry. I thought of Yubraj and Krishna again. I was ready to do it. Dipendra looked at me, waiting for my signal – red or green?

Red means I *believe* the enemy are present, and we need to throw in a grenade and clear the room. Green means it's *likely* the enemy are present. So we go in ready to fire. But no grenade. You have to make the decision in a split second, assessing the likely risk. It is always a hard one.

If you go red the enemy might run away. Or there might be children, women or the elderly in there who would be killed. Or the enemy might be using them as human shields hoping we would not hit them so hard. Equally, if we went green and the enemy were waiting inside, we could be wiped out as soon as we opened that door. So …

Red or green? An impossible call. I went green, whispering the word to Dipendra. He acknowledged with a nod. I knocked on the door. No reaction or sound. I banged harder. Still nothing. OK. I stepped back then launched myself in a flying kick at the middle of the door. (I actually did have time to feel bad about this – this was someone's house, after all, and I would not want a stranger kicking my door in. But I did not have an option.)

The door held. I had another go. And another. Still no reaction from inside. Finally the door gave way in a splintering of wood and a cloud of dust. And from inside came the loudest screams of women and children I had ever heard. The door was narrow – just enough for one person to squeeze through. I was going to send in Dipendra ahead of me. But there was maximum danger at this point.

If there was a gunman on the other side Dipendra would not stand a chance. I had to take responsibility. I signalled to him I was going in first. I got out my LLM light (with laser for use in the dark) and switched it on. The screaming from inside the room got even louder and more fearful. I took a deep breath. Counted down slowly: three, two, one … Here we go. Pointing my weapon. Dipendra right behind me.

Chaos. A room of screaming people. Faces turned away from the light, dazzled by the laser. My right finger on the trigger. Looking for enemy fighters. In this situation, all fear and adrenaline, with death just a split-second away, it would be all too easy to panic. Over-react. Squeeze that trigger. Thank God I did not.

There were no Taliban, just a group of terrified women and children. Then the next room. A huddle of women, children and old men, shocked and terrified. Their fear was a tangible thing. I tried to calm them down, apologizing in Urdu as best I could. We checked for any sign of the enemy. There were clothes, boxes, some food, nothing conclusive. I had some chocolate and money on me. I handed out bars of chocolate and a few dollars.

One of the old men pointed out of the side window, at the line of tall bamboos. He was telling us the Taliban had just escaped that way. Outside, the firefight was still in full flow. I could differentiate between friendly fire and enemy rounds because the ammunition used by each side sounded different.

I made a final apology to the civilians in the house. Handed out more chocolate and rations. Then we stepped outside into the sunlight. I saw the Platoon Commander, Lt Crawley, leading another section, ready for an assault on the other buildings we had yet to clear. Team Delta was putting down covering fire.

By now my team was really low on ammunition but we joined the forward assault. We cleared two more buildings without incident. Outside the next house a group of about fifteen fighting-age males had gathered. As we approached they just stared sullenly at us.

I really did not like the way they were looking at us. In fact it made me really angry. I was pumped up. I indicated to put their hands up. Told them to lift up their robes to make sure there were no weapons or suicide vests underneath.

My bhaiharu gave them a thorough search. Aggressive but fair, showing them who was boss.

As this was happening one of the young men kept staring at me. I did not understand what he was up to, but I had the feeling he was doing it because I was the one issuing orders. So I moved closer to him and stared back. Our eyes locked. But he could not maintain the eye-to-eye contact. He blinked and looked away. We found nothing on the search. I was convinced they were Taliban, with weapons and maybe IEDs stashed somewhere else. But we had to let them go.

By this time we were coming under only sporadic fire, so we continued to move forward. Soon we hit the line of bamboos. The enemy had vanished, leaving behind empty shell cases and rounds. This was often the frustration. We were left shadow boxing. That evening I lay on my cot bed thinking about the day. The deaths of Yubraj and Krishna guruji had never been far from my mind. I admit I had wanted revenge but the enemy had hidden like rats.

I discussed with my bhairharu what had probably happened. We had got so close to hunting them down. They had probably taken heavy casualties, and their wounded had been extracted from the front line. We could have killed a load of them. But we would never know and that was the frustrating thing. I handed out some dried meat that my wife had given me. Someone put on some Nepali music. I took out photos of my family and looked at them. My heart rate was returning to normal. I was with my brothers and we were safe. That was the main thing.

POSTSCRIPT

In November 2016, I completed my fifth and final tour of Afghanistan and returned to my family in the UK with not a scar on my body. But the thirty months I spent in some of the most dangerous combat situations of modern warfare did not leave me unscarred.

Transition to a peaceful way of life was not easy. It was hard for me to accept that danger was not just around the corner. Sudden sounds and loud bangs – even in Folkestone High Street – sent me scurrying for cover. A package lying in a doorway looked highly suspicious to me. I had trouble sleeping. Nightmares shook me awake. That was when I started getting up in the middle of the night to put my memories down on paper – and this book started to take shape.

Across the world, soldiers return from combat zones with

minds affected by traumatic events they have been involved in. The worst sufferers are diagnosed as having post-traumatic stress disorder (PTSD). For members of the British armed forces with PTSD, support is available through the MoD, the NHS and veterans' charities. I did not seek medical help. My reactions subsided within a few weeks and slowly but surely, with the help and love of my wife and children (and maybe, too, through the writing of this book), I adjusted. My life moved on.

Now I am based at Catterick Garrison in North Yorkshire where I am honoured to be in charge of the welfare of three platoons of new Gurkha recruits. I am preparing them as best I can for whatever lies ahead in their service. It is more than twenty years since I was one of them. I have come a long way in that time, from a skinny kid who had never flown in a plane before to an officer in one of the most respected fighting forces in the world.

But I remember well what it was like. The shock of how different the UK was to what I was used to in Nepal. The homesickness and how I was worried in case any of my numberi caught me crying. All the things I did not understand during training, and the questions I was afraid to ask in case I made myself look stupid.

Now I am responsible for 144 young men who will be feeling similar things. At all times I try to be humble enough to put myself in their shoes. My job is to unlock their full potential. I want to come across as a father figure rather than someone to be afraid of in case you get things wrong. After all, the

Brigade of Gurkhas is a family with a rich and proud tradition. It will be down to these young men to protect and honour the cap badge for the next generation.

One thing I know: if they turn out anything like the brothers I served with in Afghanistan they will become some of the finest soldiers and people on the planet. I will never forget those numberi, bhaiharu, sahibharu (fellow officers) and guru-ji, especially the ones who did not come back.

As I describe in the book, Yubraj Rai and Krishna Bahadur Dura were killed within two weeks of each other in 2008. One of my best and most trusted bhai, 'Gaj' – Gajbahadur Gurung – was a fine soldier who later became an NCO. In January 2012, while on deployment in the Nahr-e Saraj district of Helmand Province, he was part of a foot patrol that came under enemy fire. He took a shot to the head and was killed instantly.

There were others I knew who lost their lives in Afghanistan. They died as true Gurkhas, full of courage, noble to the end. Many were lucky to come through, like me. Some of them still serve. Others have retired. All of us share a bond of pride.

We also share memories, and these stay with me. So do the memories of the childhood brothers and sister I lost, Dhan, Santa and Benuka. They too were honourable and fearless. They taught me from a young age how to enjoy life and treat other people with love and respect. I am lucky to have had so many friends, teachers and companions in my life. But of course the person I miss most, who I owe the most to, is my mother.

A couple of years after her death I went back to our house in Charali and visited her grave in the cemetery in the forest.

I felt her presence very strongly, but this time I found it comforting. My mind went back to her final hours and minutes. The way she struggled for breath in the ambulance on her final journey home. I know she was trying to say something to me. I will never know what it was, but I can guess. She wanted to tell me not to worry, that she would be OK. It is what she used to tell me when I was growing up.

So I try not to mourn her. I imagine instead how happy she must be, surrounded by family and friends. I picture them all looking down on us, at our struggles and successes. This book is about them and for them.

GLOSSARY

Aama – Mother

ALP – Afghan Local Police

ANP – Afghan National Police

Bhaiharu – Junior colleagues

CO – Commanding Officer

CPR – Cardiopulmonary Resuscitation

C/S – Call Sign

CSgt – Colour Sergeant

CSM – Company Sergeant Major

CVR/CVRT – Combat Vehicle Reconnaissance (Tracked)

C130 – Hercules transport plane

Dai – Older brother

DC – District Centre

Dhaka topi – Nepalese cap

Dhami – Village priest

Didi – Older sister

FOB – Forward Operating Base

Guruji – Senior

HLS – Heli Landing Site

IED – Improvised Explosive Device (roadside bomb)

ILAW – Interim Lightweight Antitank Weapon

ISAF – International Security Assistance Force

ISTAR – Intelligence, Surveillance, Target Acquisition and
    Reconnaissance (battlefield intelligence gathering system)

GMG – Grenade Machine-Gun

GMLRS – Guided Multiple Launch Rocket System

GPMG – General Purpose Machine-Gun

Gurujiharu – Senior soldiers

Hesco – Temporary barrier/fortification

HMNVS – Head Mounted Night Vision System

IDF – Indirect Fire

ISAF – International Security Assistance Force

Kancha – Youngest son

Kanchi – Youngest daughter

LCpl – Lance Corporal

LMG – Light Machine-Gun

LOE – Limit of Exploitation

LSW – Light Support Weapon

Lt Col – Lieutenant Colonel

Minimi – Type of machine-gun

Murkatta – Ghost

Numberi – Contemporary/colleague

OC – Officer Commanding

OP – Observation Post

Osprey – Body armour

Pashto – Afghan language

PC – Platoon Commander

Phupu – Auntie

PRR – Personal Role Radio

PTSD – Post Traumatic Stress Disorder

QRF – Quick Reaction Force

Rfn – Rifleman

ROE – Rules of Engagement

RPG – Rocket Propelled Grenade

RUF – Revolutionary United Front (in Sierra Leone)

Sahib – Term of respect

Sahibharu – Senior officers

Sangar – Sentry post

Shamuly – Rocket flare

SOP – Standard Operating Procedure

TLZ – Tactical Landing Zone

UNMISL – United Nations Mission in Sierra Leone

VA – Vulnerable Area

VP – Vulnerable Point

WMIK – Weapons Mounted Installation Kit (armoured Land
    Rover or similar)

2IC – Second-in-command

2RGR – 2nd Battalion The Royal Gurkha Rifles

2nd Lt – Second Lieutenant

ACKNOWLEDGEMENTS

I would like to thank my father Duryodhan, my wife Sumitra and children Alisa and Anish, and my sister Indrakala: they have all always been so supportive, and shown me care, compassion and love.

My heartfelt thanks go to all my close-knit brothers in war and peace, without them I definitely would not be standing up today. Also, I am very grateful to the Brigade of Gurkha Headquarters and Ministry of Defence for their help and for giving me such a historic opportunity to publish this book.

INDEX